There are a number of books dealing with the basic techniques of karate (Kihon) and also with the set sequences of techniques of karate (Kata). There has, however, been a long felt need in karate circles for a book dealing specifically with that very important branch of karate known as free fighting (Jiyu-Kumitei). This long felt need, we are very pleased to say, has finally been met by this excellent book by Keinosuke Enoeda and Charles Mack. And we can firmly recommend 'Shotokan Karate Free Fighting Techniques' to any karate enthusiast aspiring to skill in this most challenging branch of his art.

A. Sherry,
Chairman,
Karate Union of Great Britain.

PAUL H. CROMPTON LTD.,
638 Fulham Road, London S.W.6

Magnificent Samurai — *Abelard, M.*
Basic Karate Katas — *Kanazawa, H.*
Kanku Dai — *Kanazawa, H.*
Basic Karate Katas Vol. 2 — *Smith, J.*
Competition Karate — *Valera, D.*
Introduction to Kung fu — *Jakab, L.*
Praying Mantis Kung fu — *Un, H.B.*
Nunchaku Training Manual — *MacLaren & Thompson*
Haraigoshi — *favourite judo techniques*
Seoinage — *favourite judo techniques*
Bassai Dai — Shotokan karate kata — *Anderson, J.*
Pak Mei Kung fu — *Un, H.B.*
Karate Defence and Attack — *Enoeda & Chisholm*
Karate Annuals 1 & 2 combined in one
Aikido introduction to Tomiki style — *Clapton, M.J.*
Shotokan karate free fighting techniques — *Enoeda & Mack*
Special Competition Karate — *Donovan & Valera*
Zen Combat — *Gluck, J.*
Tong Long Stick — praying mantis — *Un, H.B.*
Basic Forms of Shotokan Karate — *Anderson, J.*
Secret Techniques Wing Chun Kung Fu vol. 1 — *Chao/Weakland*
Taekwondo — *Huan, B.S.*
Primordial Pugilism, Tai Chi Chuan — *Dr. Tseng Ju Pai*
Pak Mei Tiger Fork — *Ng, J.*
Police Arrest Techniques — *Finn, M.*
Chong Woo Kwan Wing Chun — *Cheng, J.*
Beginning Ju Jitsu — *Shortt and Hashimoto*
Tomiki Aikido vol. 1 — *Dr. Lee Ah Loi*
Full Contact Martial Arts — *Warrener, D.*
Techniques of the Tonfa — *MacLaren and Thompson*
Tomiki Aikido vol. 2 — *Dr. Lee Ah Loi*
Gung Lik Kune kung fu — *Un, H.B.*
Dynamic Baton Techniques — *Wiszniewski, L.*
Secret Techniques of Wing Chun vol. 2 — *Chao/Weakland*
Fighting Fit — *MacLaren and Thompson*
Moving Zen — *Nicol*
Shukokai Karate Kata — *Morris T.*
Introduction to Shaolin Kung fu — *Wong, K.K.*
Tai Chi Weapons — *Dr. Tseng Ju Pai*

ISBN 1-874250-06-5

SHOTOKAN KARATE FREE FIGHTING TECHNIQUES

K. ENOEDA and C. J. MACK

PAUL H. CROMPTON LTD.
94, Felsham Road,
London SW 15 1dq

1 st Editon 1975

Reprinted 1985

Reprinted 1999

Reprinted 2003

Copyright © K. Eneoda & C. J. Mack 1974

Production co-ordination by

MM PRODUCTIONS LTD

1 Brookside

Hertford

Printed and Bound in Finland by Gummerus Printing Jyväskylä

Published by Paul H. Crompton Ltd. 94, Felsham Road, London SW 15 1dq

CONTENTS

Preface.

The Authors.

What Is Karate?

Guide To The Pronunciation Of The Japanese Karate Terminology.

The Different Parts Of The Hands, Arms, And Feet Used In Applying The Karate Techniques Described In This Book.

MOKUSO (MEDITATION POSTURE).

How To Use This Book.

Important Points To Remember When Engaging In Free Fighting.

Rei (Formal Salutation) And Jiyu-Dachi (Free-Fighting Stance).

15 *Chapter One. The Single, Power-House, Attacking-Technique Principle.*
Techniques employed to illustrate this principle are the following: Oi-Zuki (Lunge Punch). Gyaku-Zuki (Reverse Punch). Kizami-Zuki (Jab). Mae-Geri-Kekomi (Front Thrust Kick). Mae-Geri-Keage (Front Snap Kick). Mawashi-Geri (Roundhouse Kick). Ushiro-Geri-Kekomi (Back Thrust Kick). Ushiro-Mawashi-Geri (Back Roundhouse Kick). Yoko-Geri-Kekomi (Side Thrust Kick). Tobi-Mae-Geri (Jumping Front Kick). Tobi-Yoko-Geri (Jumping Side Kick).

31 *Chapter Two. The Pure Defence Principle.*
Techniques employed to illustrate this principle are the following: Gedan-Barai (Downward Block). Age-Uke (Rising Block). Soto-Ude-Uke (Outer Forearm Block). Ude-Barai (Forearm Sweep). Te-Nagashi-Uke (Hand-Sweeping Block). Gedan-Kake-Uke (Downward Hooking Block). Sukui-Uke (Scooping Block). Tsukamai-Uke (Grasping Block). Jodan-Shuto-Uke (Knife-Hand Block Against High Attack). Haiwan-Nagashi-Uke (Back-Arm Sweeping Block). Otoshi-Uke (Dropping Block). Ushiro-Ni-Yokeru-Koto (Retreating Evasion). Hidari-Naname-Ni-Yokeru-Koto (Left Diagonal Evasion). Migi-Naname-Ni-Yokeru-Koto (Right Diagonal Evasion).

45 *Chapter Three. The Combination-Attack Principle.*
Techniques employed to illustrate this principle are the following: Right Oi-Zuki (Lunge Punch) And Left Gyaku-Zuki (Reverse Punch). Right Oi-Zuki (Lunge Punch) And Right Yoko-Kentsui-Uchi (Side Fist-Hammer Strike). Right Oi-Zuki (Lunge Punch) And Right Mawashi-Geri (Roundhouse Kick). Right Oi-Zuki (Lunge Punch) And Right Mawashi-Geri (Roundhouse Kick) This time this combination covers a different set of circumstances to that which it covers in the preceding case. Right Mae-Geri-Kekomi (Front Thrust Kick) And Right Oi-Zuki (Lunge Punch). Left Mawashi-Geri (Roundhouse Kick) And Right Gyaku-Zuki (Reverse Punch) Left Yoko-Geri-Kekomi (Side Thrust Kick) And Right Ushiro-Mawashi-Geri (Back Roundhouse Kick) Left Yoko-Geri Kekomi (Side Thrust Kick) And Right Shuto-Uchi (Knife-Hand Strike). Right Ushiro-Geri-Kekomi (Back Thrust Kick) And Right Yoko-Ura-Ken-Uchi (Side Back-Fist Strike).

Contents

53 **Chapter Four. The Continuation-Defence Principle.**
Techniques employed to illustrate this principle are the following: Left Age-Uke (Rising Block) And Left Tsukamai-Uke (Grasping Block). Hidari-Naname-Ni-Yokeru-Koto (Left Diagonal Evasion) And Right Haiwan-Nagashi-Uke (Back-Arm Sweeping Block). Hidari-Naname-Ni-Yokeru-Koto (Left Diagonal Evasion) And Right Ude-Barai (Forearm Sweep). Ushiro-Ni-Yokeru-Koto (Retreating Evasion) And Left Gedan-Barai (Downward Block). Left Gedan-Barai (Downward Block) And Left Age-Uke (Rising Block). Right Gedan-Barai (Downward Block) And Right Soto-Ude-Uke (Outer Forearm Block). Left Te-Nagashi-Uke (Hand-Sweeping Block) And Right Gedan-Barai (Downward Block). Left Te-Nagashi-Uke (Hand-Sweeping Block) And Left Tsukamai-Uke (Grasping Block). Left Ude-Barai (Forearm Sweep) And Morote-Tate-Ude-Uke (Two-Handed Perpendicular Forearm Block).

59 **Chapter Five. The Block And Counter-Attack Principle.**
Techniques employed to illustrate this principle are the following: Left Age-Uke (Rising Block) And Right Gyaku-Zuki (Reverse Punch). Left Gedan-Barai (Downward Block) And Right Gyaku-Zuki (Reverse Punch). Right Haiwan-Nagashi-Uke (Back-Arm Sweeping Block) And Right Shuto-Uchi (Knife Hand Strike). Left Te-Nagashi-Uke (Hand-Sweeping Block) And Left Mawashi-Geri (Roundhouse Kick). Left Sukui-Uke (Scooping Block) And Right Mawashi-Zuki (Roundhouse Punch). Left Ude-Barai (Forearm Sweep) And Right Mawashi-Empi-Uchi (Roundhouse Elbow Strike). Left Ude-Barai (Forearm Sweep) And Right Ura-Zuki (Close Punch). Left Tsukamai-Uke (Grasping Block) And Right Kagi-Zuki (Hook Punch).

67 **Chapter Six. The Principle of Blocking After Attacking.**
Techniques employed to illustrate this principle are the following: Right Oi-Zuki (Lunge Punch) And Right Soto-Ude-Uke (Outer Forearm Block). Right Mae-Geri-Kekomi (Front Thrust Kick) And Right Shita-Kentsui-Uke (Downward Fist-Hammer Block). Left Mawashi-Geri (Roundhouse Kick) And Left Age-Uke (Rising Block). Left Yoko-Geri-Kekomi (Side Thrust Kick) And Left Gedan-Kake-Uke (Downward Hooking Block). Left Yoko-Geri-Kekomi (Side Thrust Kick) And Left Ude-Barai (Forearm Sweep). Right Ushiro-Geri-Kekomi (Back Thrust Kick) And Right Te-Nagashi-Uke (Hand-Sweeping Block).

73 **Chapter Seven. The Principle Of The Feint.**
Techniques employed to illustrate this principle are the following: Right Oi-Zuki (Lunge Punch) And Left Mae-Geri-Kekomi (Front Thrust Kick). Right Oi-Zuki (Lunge Punch) And Left Mawashi-Geri (Roundhouse Kick). Right Oi-Zuki (Lunge Punch) And Right Yoko-Geri-Kekomi (Side Thrust Kick). Right Ushiro-Geri-Kekomi (Back Thrust Kick) And Left Yoko-Geri-Kekomi (Side Thrust Kick). Left Yoko-Geri-Kekomi (Side Thrust Kick) And Right Ushiro-Geri-Kekomi (Back Thrust Kick). Left Mawashi-Geri (Roundhouse Kick) And Right Mae-Geri-Kekomi (Front Thrust Kick). Right Mae-Geri-Kekomi (Front Thrust Kick) And Right Oi-Zuki (Lunge Punch). Right Oi-Zuki (Lunge Punch) And Left Gyaku-Zuki (Reverse Punch).

79 **Chapter Eight. The Principle Of Throwing.**
Techniques employed to illustrate this principle are the following: De-Ashi-Barai (Advanced Foot Sweep). Kube-Nage (Neck Throw). Sode-Nage (Sleeve Throw).

List of Japanese Terms Used To Describe Karate Stances And Techniques.

List of Japanese Words And Expressions in Common Use In Karate.

ACKNOWLEDGEMENTS

The authors wish to express their thanks to Mr. Hideo Tomita, 4th Dan instructor of the Japan Karate Association and of the Karate Union of Great Britain, for allowing us to avail ourselves of his superb technique by posing in many of the technical photographs in this book.

They should also like to express their thanks to Mr. Douglas Mulquin of the London Karate Club for undertaking the difficult job of taking and processing all of the photographs in this book, the excellence of which photographs is proof of Mr. Mulquin's firm understanding both of photographic technique and also of karate technique and will undoubtedly enhance the reader's appreciation of the contents of the photographs.

We also wish to take this opportunity to express our gratitude to Mr. Andy Sherry, 4th Dan, and Mr. Terry Heaton, 4th Dan, respectively Chairman and Secretary of the Karate Union of Great Britain, and to all of the other officials and instructors of the K.U.G.B., without whose hard work over the years the large scale development and popularity of Shotokan karate in Great Britain would not have taken place, which development and popularity were largely instrumental in our deciding to write this book.

And finally our thanks are in no small measure due to the practitioners of Shotokan karate throughout the world, whose loyalty to the Shotokan style of karate has served as a great source of inspiration to us during the writing of this book.

PREFACE

The object of this book is to describe and illustrate the karate techniques and combinations of techniques which are used in the very important branch of karate training known as JIYU-KUMITE (FREE FIGHTING).

Our approach has been an analytical one so as to insure that we give as complete a treatment of our subject as it is possible to give and thus enable our readers to have a very clear understanding of this subject. And our analysis has shown quite clearly to us that the techniques and combinations of techniques of karate free-fighting can be divided into eight divisions or what we have preferred to describe as principles, being as they are of such great importance to a clear appreciation of the technical aspect of karate free fighting. And to each of these eight principles we have devoted one chapter of this book. Chapter One deals with THE SINGLE, POWER-HOUSE, ATTACKING-TECHNIQUE PRINCIPLE; Chapter Two deals with THE PURE DEFENCE PRINCIPLE; Chapter Three deals with THE CONTINUATION-ATTACK PRINCIPLE; Chapter Four deals with THE CONTINUATION-DEFENCE PRINCIPLE; Chapter Five deals with THE BLOCK AND COUNTER ATTACK PRINCIPLE; Chapter Six deals with THE PRINCIPLE OF BLOCKING AFTER ATTACKING; Chapter Seven deals with THE PRINCIPLE OF THE FEINT; and Chapter Eight deals with THE PRINCIPLE OF THROWING.

The book has been so arranged and written that it can be used profitably by all of the following: by karate teachers for the purpose of preparing their pupils for free-fighting training; by members of karate clubs who wish to improve their skill and knowledge concerning karate free-fighting techniques and combinations; and also of course by those people who though not members of a karate club are nonetheless interested in the art of karate and who would like to familiarize themselves with that very useful and fascinating branch of it which this book deals with.

We wish you every success in your endeavours:

Keinosuke Enoeda.

Charles Mack.

THE AUTHORS

KEINOSUKE ENOEDA

Keinosuke Enoeda, Karate Black Belt 7th Dan, is the official representative in Great Britain of the Japan Karate Association (J.K.A.), which association represents the Shotokan style of karate, the most widely practised style of karate in Japan. In this capacity Mr. Enoeda acts as chief instructor to the Karate Union of Great Britain (K.U.G.B.) which association represents the Shotokan style of karate in Great Britain. Mr. Enoeda is also chief instructor to the All European Karate Federation (A.E.K.F.), which federation represents the Shotokan style of karate in Europe.

He was born in the city of Fukuoka, Kyushu, Japan in 1935, and embarked upon his karate career on entering Takushoku university in Tokyo in 1953. At Takushoku, a university famous for its martial arts activities, his main karate teachers were the late Master Gichin Funakoshi, said to have been the father of Japanese karate, and Master Masatoshi Nakayama, 8th Dan and chief instructor to the Japan Karate Association and author of the best-selling book, Dynamic Karate.

After graduating from university in 1957 with a degree in commerce, Mr. Enoeda spent the next three years at the headquarters of the Japan Karate Association being trained as a teacher of karate. And at the end of this period of training he was appointed to the teaching staff of the association.

In 1961 Mr. Enoeda was placed third in the All Japan Karate Championships in Tokyo. In the following year, 1962, he was runner up in the championships. And in the next year, 1963, he won the championships to become the Japanese Karate Champion. In the same year, 1963, he also won the International Karate Championships held in Tokyo.

In 1965, with the object of spreading correct Shotokan karate, Mr. Enoeda began travelling abroad. And for a period of three years he travelled to and taught karate in countries all over the world, the countries where he spent most time being Indonesia and South Africa. Via his travels and his dynamic personality and teaching style, Mr. Enoeda has contributed greatly to the spread of Shotokan karate throughout the world and has become an internationally famous karate figure.

In 1968, Mr. Enoeda was appointed official representative in Great Britain of the Japan Karate Association and has lived in England since that time.

CHARLES MACK

Charles Mack, who runs the famous London Karate Club in Holborn, London, is one of the very few men in the world, including Japan, to be a triple Black Belt holder. He is a 3rd Dan Black Belt in Karate, J.K.A.; he is a 5th Dan Black Belt in Judo, Kodokan; and is a 1st Dan Black Belt in Aikido, Uyeshiba. He lived in Japan for seven years and is considered to be one of the world's foremost exponents and authorities on Japanese Martial Arts.

Before he left England in 1956 to emigrate to Canada, he was a leading member of the famous Budokwai Judo Club in London and held the judo grade of 3rd Dan Black Belt. He represented Britain in many international judo contests and European Championships, and is famous as being one of the few men ever to throw the Dutchman, Anton Geesink, in a judo contest. This was in the European Championships of 1955 in Paris. The Dutchman, however, landed with his back outside of the contest area so no point was awarded for the throw. Geesink later went on to become an Olympic gold medallist and also world judo champion, being the first non-Japanese ever to win this title.

After living in Canada for two years, where he practised judo at the Japanese judo club in Vancouver, British Columbia, and won the North Western Pacific Judo Championship on three different occasions, Mr. Mack left for Japan, travelling on the *Hikawa Maru*, the ship on which Doctor Jigoro Kano, the founder of Judo, had died on his return to Japan after his world tour. Mr. Mack arrived in Japan in June, 1958, and in the same year was chosen to represent Great Britain in the second World Judo Championships which were held in Tokyo in October.

After his arrival in Japan, he decided to practise Karate as well as Judo, and enrolled as a student at the Japan Karate Association's school in Yotsuya, Tokyo, at which school he practised the Shotokan style of Karate. After some years of hard training he was awarded the grade of Black Belt, making him the first British person ever to receive this grade in Japan.

He practised judo at the Kodokan, Tokyo, which is the world's leading judo school. At the Kodokan he was privileged to become a member of the Kenshusei, a special group of students receiving instruction from and training under high-grade Japanese judo masters. And after several years of hard training in both karate and judo he was awarded judo 5th Dan from the Kodokan. This is the highest judo grade ever awarded to a British person in Japan, and Mr. Mack is the only British person ever to have received this contest grade in that country.

Living only five minutes from Uyeshiba's World Aikido Headquarters in Wakamatsu-Cho, Tokyo, he also had opportunity to practise Aikido, in which martial art he also progressed to Black Belt grade.
Since leaving Japan, he has been prominent in Japanese martial arts activities in Britain. He is an ex-member of the British Judo Association's Technical Board, and is also a senior examiner of that association. He is also chief karate instructor at The London Karate Club in Holborn, London.

WHAT IS KARATE?

Karate is a system of unarmed combat, practised as a highly competitive sport, in which the participants specialize mainly in kicking, punching and striking techniques, and blocking and defensive movements to same.

It originated in China some hundreds of years ago, from which country it found its way to Okinawa. It was introduced to Japan in the early part of the present century by various experts from Okinawa, including Gichin Funakoshi, who is said to have been the father of Japanese karate. He was also the founder of the Shotokan school of karate, which style is practised by the Japan Karate Association. Funakoshi died in April, 1957, at the age of eighty eight.

In karate, a white uniform of light cloth, consisting of a hip-length jacket, ankle-length pants, and a cloth belt to keep the jacket intact, is worn. The wearing of a jacket facilitates the application of some of the techniques which are practised, and the belt also indicates the grade of the wearer.

In karate, as in many Japanese activities, a grading system is used. That is, grades are awarded to indicate the degree of proficiency a person has reached in the art. There are two kinds of grades: Kyu grades and Dan grades. Literally, Kyu means step, whereas Dan means degree. As can be gathered by these two meanings, the kyu grades are lower than the dan grades. The kyu grades range from 9th kyu, which is the lowest, to 8th kyu, 7th kyu, 6th kyu, 5th kyu, 4th kyu, 3rd kyu, 2nd kyu, and finally to 1st kyu, which is the highest kyu grade. In Japan one wears a white belt until one progresses to 3rd kyu, then from 3rd kyu to 1st kyu a brown belt is worn. In Britain, however, most clubs have a coloured belt system for kyu grades almost similar to that in judo. Although the system may vary from club to club, the following is rather typical: white belt with 9th kyu, yellow belt with 8th kyu, orange belt with 7th kyu, green belt with 6th kyu, blue belt with 5th kyu, purple belt with 4th kyu, and brown belt from 3rd kyu to 1st kyu. The next step on the promotion ladder is from the highest of the kyu grades, 1st kyu, to the lowest of the dan grades, 1st dan. The dan grades are the Black Belt Grades because the person with a dan grade always wears a black belt while wearing his karate uniform. The dan grades range from 1st dan, 2nd dan, 3rd dan, and finally to 4th dan, which is usually the highest grade given for fighting proficiency. After 4th dan, promotion to 5th dan and even higher can be gained for contributions to the art, such as in the case of a clever, productive teacher, or an original thinker who has brought about innovations for the betterment of the sport.

In karate, there are two types of contest: grading contests, where one will attempt to prove one's proficiency in order to gain promotion to a higher grade; and championship contests, where one participates, as in any other sport, to win the championship, or at least to get a good place. At the latter, as in all sporting events, medals, cups, shields, etc., are presented to the victor and the runners-up. The length of an individual match will vary according to its importance, but in the main, a match will last three minutes with extensions of one minute, two minutes, or three minutes in the case of a drawn result. Again, the length of the extension will usually be determined by the importance of the match. Usually three of these extensions will be permitted and then if neither of the participants has been able to gain a points advantage over the other, the referee and the four judges will award one of them a superiority win-although occasionally a draw is given. Most karate matches are one point matches, and the man to score with a powerful attacking technique which the referee considers worth a full point wins the match, and the match is terminated there and then. If, however, it is adjudged that the technique used was just not strong enough to warrant a full point, then a half point may be awarded. If a man is awarded two half points in this manner, he will be adjudged winner of the match and it will be terminated. And even if he does not manage to convert his first half point into a full point by the scoring of another half point, at the end of the contest he will almost always be awarded the decision for his half point lead. Sometimes, however, in spite of his half point lead at the end of the match, the match may be declared a draw, or the match could even be awarded to the other man.

This can happen when the man with the half point lead has been given a warning for some infringement of the rules, or if he has cancelled his half point lead by negative or extremely defensive play.

Usually, in the case of team matches, no extension in the case of a drawn match will be given. At the end of a match, a draw will be declared and the next match will commence.

Regarding the infringement of the rules of karate contest, the guilty party, in the case of a serious infringement, will be immediately disqualified. In the case of an infringement which is not of a serious nature, however, he will not be disqualified but will be given a warning. This means that if he infringes the rules again, however, seriously or otherwise, he will be disqualified. And even if he does not infringe the rules a second time, the fact that he has been given a warning will be to his disadvantage if at the end of the match a superiority decision has to be given.

GUIDE TO JAPANESE PRONUNCIATION

Although the karate terminology is in Japanese. it is very easy to pronounce if you follow the few following simple little rules.

In the case of the vowels, that is the letters *a*, e, i, o, u, always pronounce them in the following manner, which is the only way they are ever pronounced: pronounce *a* like the a in the word *at*; pronounce *e* like the *e* in the word *egg*; pronounce *i* like the *e* in the word b*e*; pronounce *o* like the word *awe*; and pronounce *u* like the *o* in the word d*o*.

In the case of the double vowel *ei*, its pronunciation has no equivalent in standard English, but is to be pronounced as the *ay* is pronounced in words like n*ay* in the Yorkshire dialect.

In the case of the letter *y*, it is never pronounced like the letter *i* as it is often pronounced in English in words like cr*y*, but is always pronounced like the *y* in *y*es.

In the case of the letter *g*, it can be pronounced like the *g* in *g*o and also like the *ng* in words like bri*ng*, ki*ng*, si*ng*, etc., but is never pronounced like the *g* in words like *g*entle. In fact, in this book, the letter *g*, with the exception of the *g* in the words *gedan, geta, go, gohon,* and *gyaku*, always has its *ng* pronunciation. In the case of these exceptions, the *g* is pronounced, therefore, like the *g* in the word *g*o.

The other letters in the karate terminology are to be pronounced as they are in English words.

You can see, therefore, just how easy a thing it is to pronounce correctly the words in the karate terminology. However, at first, until you feel that you have learnt the above rules for the correct pronunciaton of the karate terminology, keep referring to this section each time that you come across a new karate term in order to enable you to give it its correct pronunciation.

THE DIFFERENT PARTS OF THE BODY

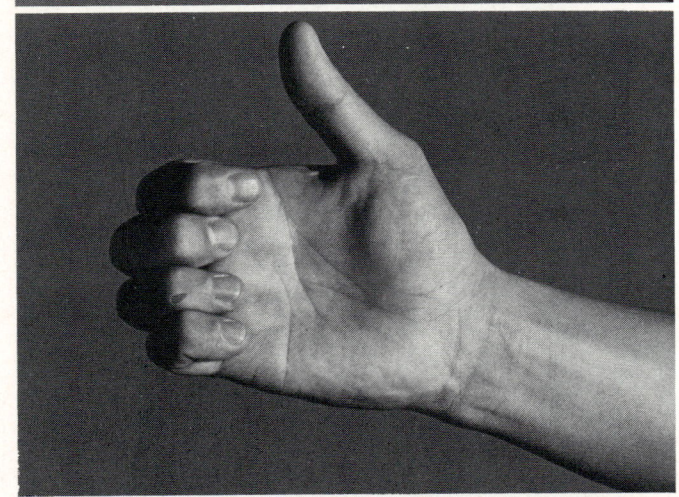

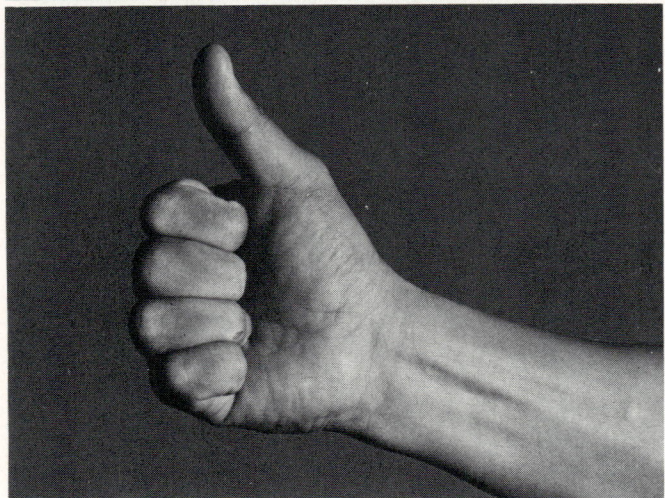

THE DIFFERENT PARTS OF THE HANDS, ARMS, AND FEET USED IN APPLYING THE KARATE TECHNIQUES DESCRIBED IN THIS BOOK.

HANDS AND ARMS

SEIKEN (FORE-FIST). Photo 5.
Used in punching techniques.
URAKEN (BACK-FIST). Photo 6.
Used for striking.
KENTSUI (HAND-HAMMER). Photo 7.
Used for both striking and blocking.
SHUTO (KNIFE-HAND). Photo 8.
Used for both striking and blocking.
SHO (PALM). Photo 9.
Used for blocking.
EMPI (ELBOW). Photo 10.
Used for striking.
GAIWAN (OUTER-ARM). Photo 11.
Used for blocking.
HAIWAN (BACK-ARM). Photo 12.
Used for blocking.
NAIWAN (INNER-ARM). Photo 13.
Used for blocking.

HOW TO FORM A FIST

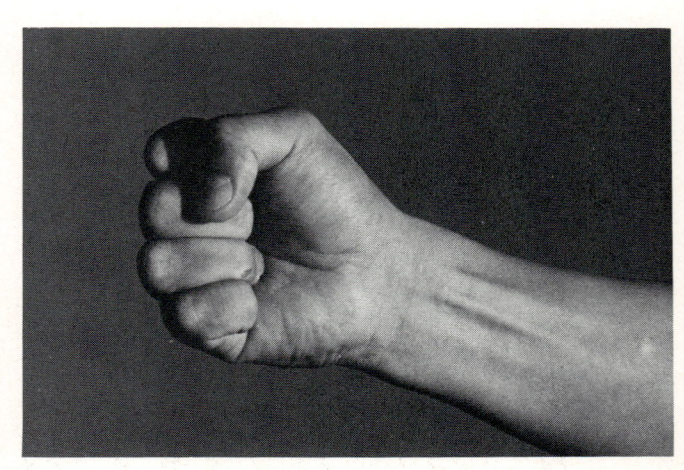

Bend all of the fingers at the middle joint so that the tips of the fingers are pressed firmly against the roots of the fingers (Photos 1 & 2). Now clench the hand, bending it at the knuckles joint and also by pressing the heel of the hand. (Photo 3). Squeeze firmly the index finger and the middle finger with your thumb, thus ensuring that these fingers and the thumb are firmly secure in a way which will afford them the greatest protection from injury. (Photo 4).

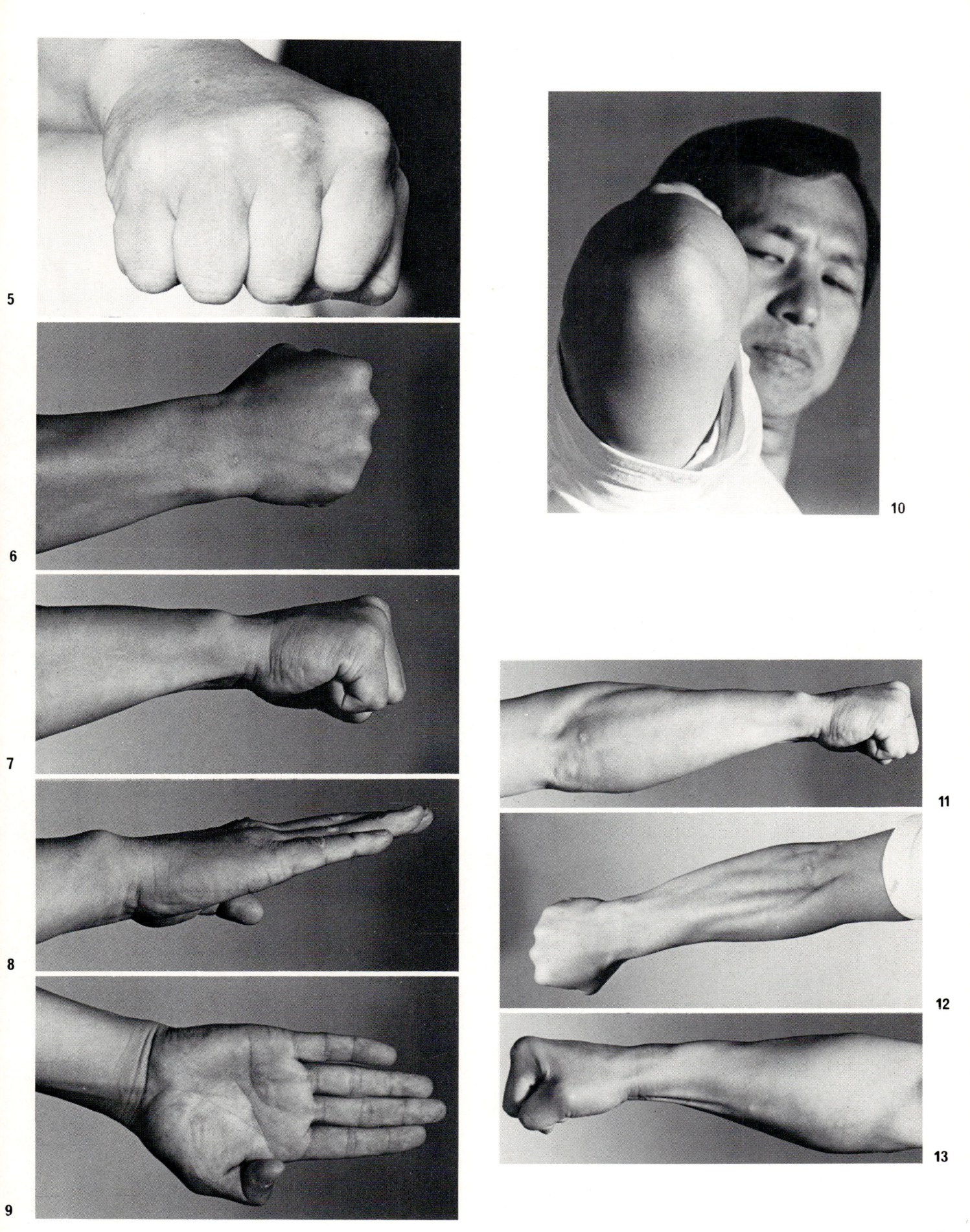

5

6

7

8

9

10

11

12

13

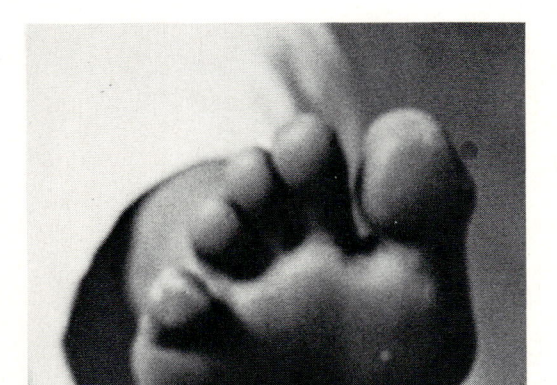

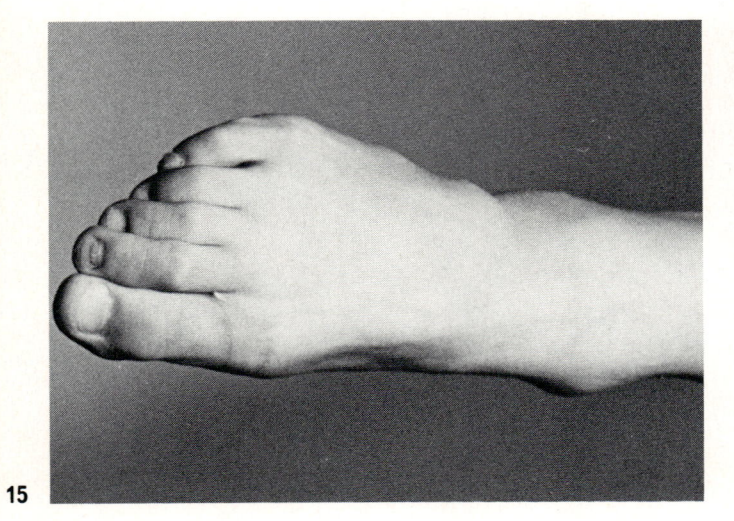

FEET

KOSHI (BALL OF THE FOOT). Photo 14.
Used for Front Kicking and Roundhouse Kicking.
HAISOKU (INSTEP). Photo 15.
Used for Roundhouse Kicking as an alternative to using the ball of the foot.
SOKUTO (FOOT EDGE). Photo 16.
Used in Side Kicking.
KAKATO (HEEL). Photos 17 and 18.
The bottom of the heel (Photo 17) is used in Back Kicking. And the back of the heel (Photo 18) is used in Back Roundhouse Kicking.

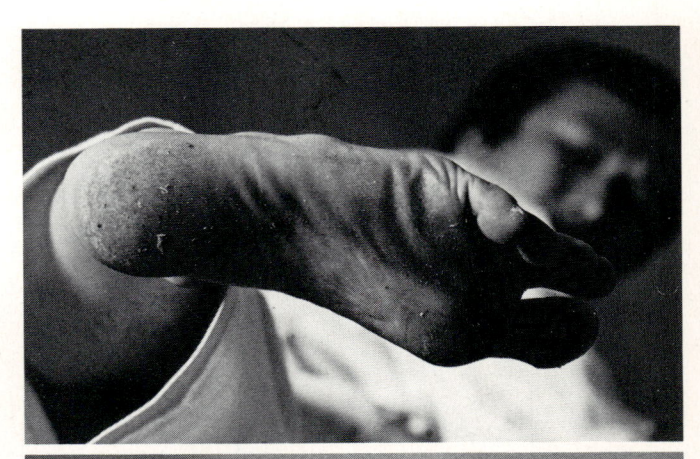

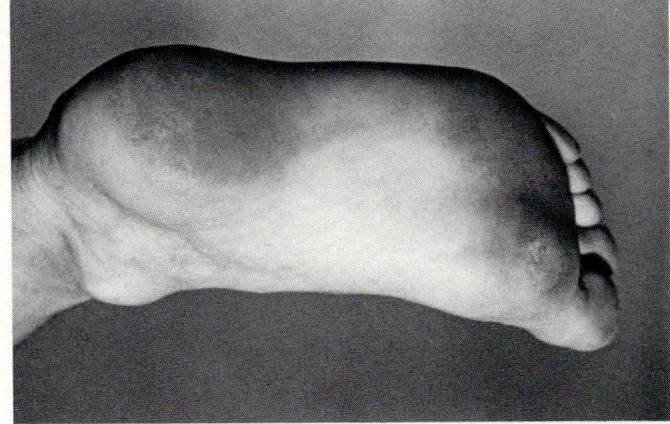

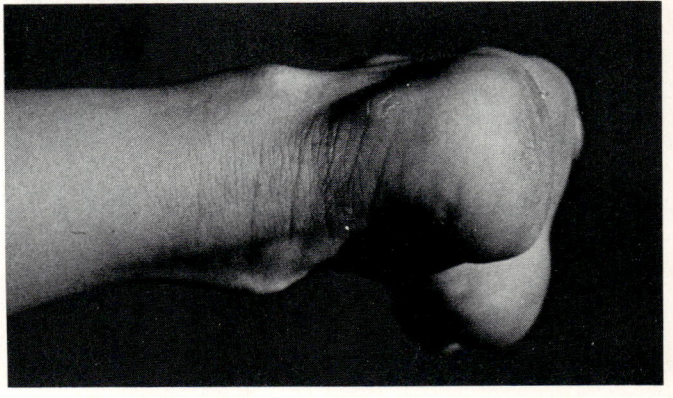

MOKUSO

This is the posture taken up after a training session. The idea is to remain in this position for a minute or so with the eyes closed, body relaxed, and mind free from distracting thoughts, and to try to attain to a state of calmness free from any tension or thoughts of aggression which the training might have brought on.

The Mokuso posture is taken up in the following way:

1. Take up the position shown in Photo 19.
2. Place your left knee to the ground in front of you. Photo 20.
3. Place your right knee to the ground in front of you. Photo 21.
4. Finally, placing your insteps flat on the floor behind you, place the top of your left foot over the sole of your right foot and sit on your heels. Photo 22. Photo 23 shows the position of the feet. Photo 24 shows the same final posture with the eyes closed. Photo 25 shows a permitted alternative foot position where instead of the top of the left foot being placed over the sole of the right foot, the top of the left big toe is placed over the bottom of the right big toe. This is a much easier and comfortable position to take up for beginners.

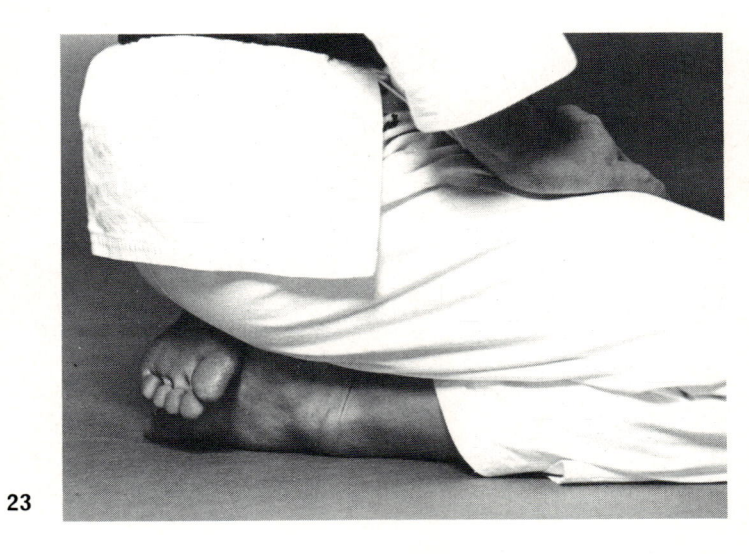

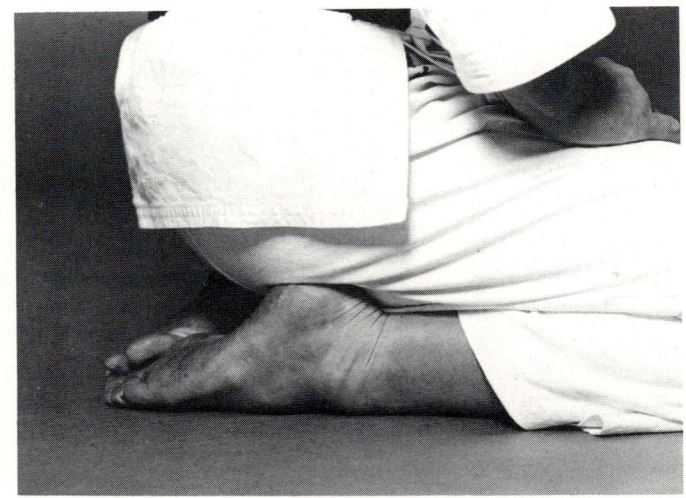

22

23

24

25

HOW TO USE THIS BOOK

Actual free-fighting should only be done under qualified supervision at your club. The techniques themselves can be practised by two people quite safely under pre-arranged conditions, using the text and illustrations in this book and heeding the following advice and instructions.

Traditionally karate training is done in bare feet. But, if practising on a rough surface you are advised to wear some kind of soft footwear.

Practise frequently and regularly but no more than about thirty minutes a day at first, gradually increasing the length of time as your body becomes used to the activity. Thus you will avoid the risk of straining your muscles, tendons, etc. You will also avoid losing the enthusiasm for the activity brought about by over-practising at first. When applying the techniques be careful not to actually strike your opponent but stop just short of the mark, as it were. When practising the throwing techniques in the last chapter, extreme care should be taken. If not, injury to your partner can result.

First study the FORMAL SALUTATION (REI) and the FREE-FIGHTING STANCE (JIYU-DACHI) described and illustrated before the first chapter. Next, after reading and studying up to the first technique, Oi-zuki, (Lunge Punch), begin with a partner to practise this technique in conjunction with studying the technique via the text and illustrations. The main performer in each photo illustrating the techniques is on the left of the reader.

Do not practise too long or too violently at first. Be content with twenty repetitions of the movement involved, in this case the Lunge Punch. Your partner then does the same thing. Following the directions given above move on to the next technique, doing twenty repetitions, then returning to the first technique. Progress in this way through chapter one. If you train in this way, by the time you reach the end of chapter one you and your partner will have developed a good degree of skill in executing these first techniques.

Then move on to chapter two, progressing in the same manner as in chapter one, leaving techniques in chapter one alone until you have consolidated those of chapter two. Then return and revise chapter one, before moving on and dealing in the same way with chapter three. Go through the whole book in this way.

IMPORTANT POINTS TO REMEMBER

Although it is better ideally to practise with a partner, if one is not available, one can derive a great deal of benefit from practising the techniques alone, using an imaginary partner instead of a real one.

1. When facing your opponent or manouvering in free fighting, it is advisable to keep your hands closed, except when you have to open your hands for blocking or striking. This will prevent your getting the fingers hurt if the hands make strong contact accidentally with your opponent's foot, fist, etc. Do not keep the fists strongly clenched, as this will tire the arms. Simply clench the fists so that the forearm muscles are only slightly contracted.

2. When sparring keep approximately three feet separating the front of your leading foot from the front of your opponents' leading foot. This distance will enable you both to attack and defend yourself adequately. If you stand too near each other there is a tendency for the activity to become too rough and also the skill otherwise required in free-sparring is considerably reduced. One should avoid standing too far from each other as this renders the activity rather unrealistic.

3. When aiming blows to the opponent's face or other bony structures it is not permitted to actually hit. One must therefore execute an attack with control, so that one can stop the blow just short of the mark. In order to do this well good distancing is required. Not too near nor too far from the opponent. This aspect of karate free-fighting is called 'ma-ai', which does simply mean 'distancing'. One should give a lot of thought to it. In the case of aiming blows at the diaphram and stomach, which areas can be contracted to afford protection, it is permitted to make contact but even so one should not apply excessive force when delivering an attacking technique.

4. To make karate free-fighting possible, blows that are lower than the stomach are not permitted. Nor is one permitted to aim at the eyes, **or throat** especially with poking type techniques with the open fingers. If for some reason an opponent's back is turned, blows may be aimed at his back, head or back of the neck, but it is not permitted to allow such blows to make contact. This could easily damage the kidneys, spine, etc., which is to be avoided at all costs.

5. It is advisable, until one gets quite a lot of experience, to wear pads on the bony parts of the arms, just above the wrist bones, and also on the front of the shin. These parts of the arms and legs are the most open to bruising. The ulnar nerve on the inside of the elbow is also vulnerable and if this part is frequently caught a pad should be worn there too. Experienced or not one should wear a crutch protector in free-fighting. The most common type is a jock strap with a little pocket in front into which a plastic shield-shaped protector is placed.

6. When engaging in free fighting it is best to have a third man acting as arbitrator. If not practicable then adopt the following measures. If one thinks an opponent has scored, then acknowledge it. This is done simply by shouting out 'point', and stopping the action. Then the participants move three feet away from each other and the one against whom the point has been scored counts to six, then **calls** 'right' to his opponent. At this juncture the match begins again. This will ensure that the free-fighting does not degenerate into a non-stop, scrambling, disorganised affair, but is practised in a reasonable, controlled fashion.

Rei
(Formal Salutation)

REI (FORMAL SALUTATION)

First, face your opponent, each of you in the Open Leg Stance (Hachiji-Dachi), with a distance of approximately seven feet separating you. (Photo 26).

Second, bringing first your left foot to your centre and then your right foot to your left foot, stand with both heels together with your feet pointing outwards at forty-five degrees and with the palms of your hands on your thighs. (photo 27)

Thirdly, bow to each other. (Photo 28), then return to the upright position in photo 27.

Fourthly, moving first your left foot then your right foot out to their respective sides, cross your arms in front of you (Photo 29), and then uncross them to return to the Open Leg Stance, (Photo 30).

JIYU-DACHI (FREE-FIGHTING STANCE)

This is the stance in which you and your opponent face each other when engaged in free-fighting and therefore the stance from which you must learn how to execute all the techniques described in this book.

On completing the Formal Salutation described above, you than take up the free-fighting stance in the following manner. Advance your left foot about two feet towards your opponent, keeping your left foot further out to your left than your right foot and turning your left heel outwards about thirty degrees. Your right foot should be pointed approximately in the same direction as your left foot and both knees should be slightly bent. Your left fist is thrust forward level with your solar plexus, the left arm is slightly bent at the elbow. Your right fist should be thrust about six inches in front of you and held only slightly lower than your left fist. Your body should be turned to your right, away from your opponent at forty-five degrees, and your fists should be also turned outwards from the perpendicular forty-five degrees. This enables you to use them to their best advantage for both punching and blocking. It is also important to preserve an upright position so as to execute movements in a well-balanced and controlled fashion.

The distance separating you from your opponent after each of you moves his left foot approximately two feet forward when assuming the free-fighting stance should be approximately three feet, which distance will enable you to apply attacks without finishing up either too near or too far from each other on completing these attacks. (Photo 31).

(Photo 32 gives a front view of the free-fighting stance).

Jiyu-Dachi

CHAPTER 1

The Single Power-House Attacking Technique Principle

INTRODUCTION

In karate free-fighting, if you can score with a powerful technique as your first move, then you have achieved your object and that is all there is about it. To make this clearer, you must realise that very often you will score with a continuous attack after your first technique has been nullified in some way, or you may score after first blocking your opponent's attack or after having evaded it in some way, and so on. In other words, making more than one move to achieve your object. To illustrate this single, power-house, attacking-technique principle, which is the principle upon which the art of karate is based and to which all other principles are secondary, we have chosen the following techniques, as they are the ones which allow one to practise this principle with most frequency when engaged in free-fighting:

Oi-zuki, Gyaku-zuki, Kizami-zuki, Mae-geri-kekomi, Mae-geri-keage, Mawashi-geri, Ushiro-geri-kekomi, Ushiro-mawashi-geri, Yoko-geri-kekomi.

Oi-Zuki

INTRODUCTION

'Oi' means 'Lunge' and 'Zuki' means 'Punch', thus referring to the lunging action of the body involved in this punch.

This technique is one which is essential to everyone aspiring to excellence in free-fighting. Not only is it a powerful attacking technique but it is also a major technique. This means that a large body movement is required for its performance. By frequent practise of 'oi-zuki' you can familiarise your body and mind with the dynamic movement on which karate is based. It is also true that minor techniques using smaller body movements are also dynamic but to a lesser extent, obviously. So, major techniques more readily familiarise a student with the dynamism of karate. Major and minor techniques are required for an all-round karate free-fighting knowledge, but you must give a lot of time and thought to acquiring a powerful and skilful 'oi-zuki'.

TECHNICAL DESCRIPTION

Face your opponent in the free-fighting stance. (Photo 1) Without moving your hands and keeping the body upright lunge at your opponent by stepping directly towards him with the right foot. (Photo 2).

Without a pause continue stepping towards him and simultaneously punch by thrusting the front of your right fist with an anti-clockwise twisting motion at him, so that you complete the punch with your right arm fully extended and with the back of your right fist facing up as you complete your stepping action, your right foot firmly planted on the floor close to your opponent. The left fist is withdrawn to your left hip. (Photo 3).

NOTES

1. A large step is required for this punch therefore it must be carried out with great speed and determination so that the opponent cannot step back out of range.
2. The left hand should be kept well in front of you as you lunge towards your opponent, to block any attacking technique the opponent may attempt to use against you as you lunge towards him and before you have time to complete the punch.

Gyaku-Zuki

INTRODUCTION

'Gyaku' means 'reverse' or 'opposite'.

In karate 'gyaku' refers to the same side of the body as the rear foot, and the opposite side to that of the front foot. So if you stand in the orthodox free-fighting stance with left foot leading, and punch with the right hand from that stance you are said to be using the 'opposite' hand; right gyaku-zuki. Switch the hand and foot positions and you are doing a left gyaku-zuki. A more precise equivalent in English of 'gyaku-zuki' would be 'opposite side punch' or 'rear hand punch.

Gyaku-zuki is a very useful punch, allowing a karate player to use it for the purpose of positive attack, and also for counter punching after blocking an opponent's attack. For these reasons it is the most popular punching technique in the karate repertoire. It is worth practising and thinking in detail about this most essential technique.

TECHNICAL DESCRIPTION

Face your opponent as in Photo 1. Step towards him to get within range. (Photo 4). Without pausing allow the right foot to follow behind the left and punch at the same time by thrusting the front of your right clenched fist with an anti-clockwise twisting action at your opponent's face area, completing the punch with the back of the fist facing up, arm fully extended as your right foot is firmly planted behind your left. The left fist is withdrawn to your left hip. (Photo 5). Photo 6 shows the punch being delivered to the solar plexus.

NOTES

1. As you step and before you punch keep your left arm ahead of you to block any attack made before you can deliver the punch.
2. Do not allow the body to rise as you step left-foot-right-foot. This increases the stepping time, enabling the opponent to step out of range, and increases your buoyancy, which an alert opponent would turn to his advantage.
3. You may find yourself close enough to perform a gyaku-zuki without the step, as for instance after you have blocked an opponent's attack. This kind of situation will be dealt with later; but in most cases it is necessary to first step towards an opponent, reducing the distance normally separating you in free-fighting.

Kizami-Zuki

INTRODUCTION

'Kizami' in fact means 'to chop into little pieces, and 'zuki' as said before means 'punch'. The free translation is best made by the word 'jab'; the full term of 'kizami-zuki' being 'jabbing punch', or briefly 'jab'.

It is not such a powerful punch as the two main straight punching techniques, oi-zuki and gyaku-zuki, nor does it enable you to score as many points but your karate arsenal would be incomplete without it.

Though kizami-zuki can be used to good effect when one is positioned quite close to an opponent, or after the rear hand (right) has blocked an attack, it is used as a point scorer in the role of a stopper. A 'stopper' is used to stop an opponent as he lunges towards you, reducing the effect of his attack, and at the same time giving you a point. When developed, kizami-zuki is a formidable deterrent to people who excel in the lunging type of attack. (**A** 'stopper' is its main use.)

TECHNICAL DESCRIPTION

Face your opponent as in Photo 1. Step towards him to reduce the distance, with your left foot, and at the same time bend the punching arm to give impetus to the punching left hand. (Photo 7). Without pausing, continue stepping towards the opponent with the left foot and simultaneously thrust the front of your left clenched fist with a clockwise twisting action at the opponent so that the punch is completed with the back of the fist facing up and left arm fully extended, as the left foot is firmly planted on the floor close to him. The body is twisted to your right and your right fist is withdrawn to your right hip. (Photo 8).

NOTES

1. As this punch is done with the hand in front it is not possible to introduce as much power into it as in the case of punches with the rear hand. One cannot use the lunging action of oi-zuki nor the powerful body-twisting action of gyaku-zuki to add force to the punch. Kizami-zuki is done with the leading hand however, and can therefore be done **speedily**, and containing the element of surprise. In karate free-fighting the element of surprise is important, and so the ability to use kizami-zuki can serve one very well in this activity.

Kizami-Zuki

10

TECHNICAL DESCRIPTION OF KIZAMI-ZUKI USED AS A "STOPPER".

As your opponent moves towards you to deliver his attack using for example oi-zuki, step towards him with your left foot and do kizami-zuki in exactly the same way as described above. (Photo 9). Very often, when using kizami-zuki as a 'stopper' it is not always possible, due to the opponent's having moved very close to you for his attack, to give additional force to your punch by stepping towards him. In this case, simply deliver the kizami-zuki without making the stepping action. (Photo 10).

NOTES
1. Due to the speed with which kizami-zuki must be used as a 'stopper', usually one does not have time to give an additional bend to the punching arm in order to add impetus to the punch, but must be content merely to straighten the arm from the position in which it is held in the free-fighting stance. This contrasts with the position where kizami-zuki is used as a positive, attacking technique, with enough time to give additional force to the punch by increasing the bend in the punching arm before delivering the punch.

Mae-Geri-Kekomi

INTRODUCTION

'Mae' means 'front', 'geri' means 'kick', 'kekomi' means 'thrust'. This term refers to the fact that when this kick is applied the front of the body is facing the target and the leg is used in a thrusting fashion, as distinct from the other style of karate kick which uses the snapping action of the knee.

Mae-geri-kekomi is used widely by beginners to karate because of the comparative simplicity with which it can be executed. For exactly the same reason it is used a great deal by karate players with a wealth of experience. Simplicity of execution does not prevent a technique from being developed to such a point that it is not included in the repertoire of an experienced karate player. On the contrary, there is no doubt that when this kick is done correctly and with power it is useful even against an experienced karate man.

The great advantage of a well executed front **thrust** kick is that it enables you to cover a lot of distance, straight forward, as opposed to upward, with your kicking foot. Its simplicity means that it can be done quickly, and these two factors indicate its effectiveness against an opponent standing some distance from you. As many karate players frequently adopt the tactic of standing out of range of techniques, the skilful use of mae-geri-kekomi will enable you to combat such measures.

TECHNICAL DESCRIPTION

Face opponent as in Photo 1. Pushing all your weight forward on to your left leg, your left hand kept well forward and drawing your right hand back to your right side, thrust your right knee forward and up, while turning your right foot and toes up. (Photo 11). Without stopping the momentum of your movement and preserving your hand position, keep the front of your body facing your opponent and thrust the ball of your right foot with a powerful extension of your right leg straight at him. (Photo 12).
Photo 13 shows the kick being directed at the upper-level target area.

NOTES

1. The left hand forward and the right hand back keeps the body from twisting to the left and so facing forward, which is the best position for delivering this kick with maximum power. The left hand can also be used for blocking and the right for punching, should the need arise.

Mae-Geri-Kekomi

14

15

MAE-GERI-KEKOMI USED AS A "STOPPER"

Due to the speed with which a technique used as a stopper has to be delivered, when kicking techniques are employed for this purpose, it is usually the front foot which is used.

TECHNICAL DESCRIPTION

Face your opponent as in Photo 1. As the opponent moves towards you to attack using for example an oi-zuki, push your left foot into the air, turning the foot and toes up, as you take your weight on your right leg. (Photo 14). Then with speed and determination thrust the ball of your left foot straight at your opponent by forcefully straightening your left leg and stop him in his tracks. The left arm is straightened and the right fist drawn back. (Photo 15).

NOTES

1. Begin the kick before the opponent gets too near you so that when you complete the kick the left leg is completely tensed in the fully extended position, which is the only position which will enable you to stop a strong opponent in his tracks. If you begin as your opponent is too near you will not be able to complete the kick correctly. You will also be in a weak position, balanced only on one leg. **and at a serious disadvantage as this position is good neither for executing an attacking nor a defending technique with much power.**

2. When the foot is used as a stopper emphasis must be placed on directing it forward as distinct from upward, as obviously a forward emphasis with your foot is the only one which will enable you to offer the maximum degree of resistance to your opponent. This is because his oncoming movement is directly opposite to your kick. This does on the other hand afford you the best possible chance of halting your opponent's progress towards you.

Mae-Geri-Keage

INTRODUCTION

The word 'keage' is derived from the first syllable of 'keru', which means 'to kick', and the word 'age' which means 'upwards' or 'rising'. 'Keage' therefore means literally 'to kick upwards'. Because of the snapping action of the knee, when doing upward kicks, the word 'keage' is usually translated by the word 'snap'.

The Front Snap Kick is similar to the Front Thrust Kick (Mae-Geri-Kekomi) in the sense that the front of the body is facing in the same direction as the kick. The difference in these two techniques is that the main function of the Front Thrust Kick is to enable you to make contact with an opponent standing at quite a distance. The main function of the Front Snap Kick is to cover distance upwards, and is therefore a better kick to use than the latter when aiming high at the opponent's face. This is brought about by the snapping action of the knee in this style of kicking, which facilitates the gaining of height.

TECHNICAL DESCRIPTION

Assume the stance of Photo 1. Push all your weight on to your left leg, left hand thrust forward and right hand back, and thrust your right knee forward and up while stretching your right foot down but curling your right toes up. (Photo 16).

Without interrupting the momentum of your movement and preserving your hand position, keep the front of your body facing the opponent and with a snapping, relaxed action of the right knee, aim the ball of your right foot upwards at your opponent's chin. (Photo 17).

NOTES

1. For the same reasons as those given in the note on Mae-geri-kekomi keep the left hand well forward and the right hand pulled back.

Mawashi-Geri

INTRODUCTION

'Mawashi' means 'circular' or 'round', and 'geri' means 'kick'. In English this technique has come to be known as the 'roundhouse kick'. The name of this technique refers to the fact that in its performance the leg moves in a circular fashion.

Mawashi-geri has everything which appeals to the karate man. It is first and foremost a technique which can be done with a lot of power; it requires for its execution an athletic movement and grace. That it is undoubtedly a stylish technique plays no little part in its being so popular. Add to these attributes the fact that Mawashi-geri is one of the major point-scoring techniques in karate contests and you will appreciate the importance of including it in your bag of free-fighting techniques.

TECHNICAL DESCRIPTION

Assume the stance of Photo 1. Pivoting to your right on the ball of your left foot and pushing all your weight on that foot, raise your right leg simultaneously sideways and forwards high into the air, while pulling your right heel close to the back of your right thigh and turning your right foot and toes up. (Photo 18). Without interrupting the momentum of your movement direct the ball of your right foot towards your opponent by straightening your right leg in a circular fashion with the outside of the leg facing upwards. At the same time continue to pivot on the ball of your left foot and twist your torso to your left. To check the circling action of the kick to concentrate its force on the target in front of you, it is advisable, until you become fairly expert, to direct the arm on the same side as the kicking leg to your rear. The other hand for the same reason is kept in front of you. (Photo 19).

NOTES

1. Mawashi-geri is also often done with the top of the foot instead of the ball of the foot, and this will be shown in the next article. Kicking with the ball of the foot is considered more powerful but kicking with the top of the foot reduces the chance of damage to the toes. Practise of both methods will enable you to appreciate the advantages and disadvantages of both.

MAWASHIGERI WITH THE FOOT IN FRONT

Step towards your opponent with your right foot by taking it slightly past your left foot, toes out to the right a little. Hand positions do not change. (Photo 20). The technique is then the same as described for the rear foot, using the top of the foot. Direct the kick to the target with a high circular action of the leg, position the arms by directing your left arm to the rear and keeping your right hand in front. (Photo 21).

NOTES

1. The step is not necessary if you are close enough to your opponent already. For instance, after you have blocked an attack from him.

Ushiro-Geri-Kekomi

INTRODUCTION

'Ushiro' means 'back' or 'rear'. 'Geri' and 'kekomi' we know already. When this kick is applied the back of the body is facing the target and the leg is used in a thrusting fashion. This technique is undoubtedly the most powerful in the karate repertoire. Because the large, fast and well-timed movement required in its execution develops one's athletic potential it is highly desirable as a technique in free-fighting. Ushiro-Geri-Kekomi is difficult at first, but it is surprising how quickly with practice one can do it quite well. Then you realise just how useful it can be and it is at this point you have the incentive to continue your practice until you do the kick with control and expertise. More and more power can be introduced at this stage till finally you have such a devastating kick that you will need to exert great care in using it except against a very experienced karate player.

Ushiro-Geri-Kekomi is additionally useful as it gives you the ability to deliver techniques from every conceivable angle, when combined with the other techniques which you are learning. It can be used in the combination and feinting techniques which are a part of free-fighting methods.

22

23

TECHNICAL DESCRIPTION

Assume the stance of Photo 1. Position yourself by turning your back to your opponent, for the kick, which is done by pivoting clockwise on the ball of your left foot, pushing the weight of your body towards your left leg, and glancing over your right shoulder. (Photo 22). Then, with your back to your opponent, bend your right leg and thrust the bottom of your right heel at him by forcefully straightening your right leg. In delivering the kick, thrust your right arm to your rear and bring your left fist close to your body. This position of the hands will not interfere with the naturalness of the kicking action to the rear. (Photo 23).

NOTES
1. To succeed with Ushiro-Geri-Kekomi the pivot on the left leg, the weight shift, must both be done with speed and smoothness. Without this speed an opponent will be able to retreat out of range before you can complete it.
2. Avoid letting the right side of your body twist too far towards the opponent. This increases the time taken for the kick; so keep your back towards him all through the kick, executing it in the shortest time.

INTRODUCTION

We already know the meaning of the separate words making up this technique: 'ushiro'-'back', 'mawashi'-'circular', 'geri'-'kick'. In English the expression 'back roundhouse kick' is used. The foot moves in a circular action to the rear. Once you have learned Ushiro-Geri-Kekomi, thereby getting used to turning your back on your opponent, you can easily, with some adaptation, learn to do Back Roundhouse Kick.

Though not as powerful as the Back Thrust Kick this technique has many advantages. Its use of a circular action enables you to attack via an indirect route, which is more difficult to defend against than a direct attack, especially when done at high speed. It is also easy to employ in a high level attack. It has the added value of being easy to turn into after say your attacking left leg has been turned aside by an opponent's block. As this happens quite often the usefulness of learning the Back Circular Kick is very clear. The fact that one can quite easily move into a lot of interesting karate techniques after first doing this kick makes it an extremely useful and quite fascinating karate movement.

TECHNICAL DESCRIPTION.

Assume the stance in Photo 1. Position yourself by turning your back to your opponent by pivoting clockwise on the ball of the left foot, pushing the weight of your body on to the left leg, and glancing over your right shoulder. (Photo 24). Continuing the momentum of your movement without interruption, start moving your right leg in a circular fashion to your rear and upwards. (Photo 25). Finally, aim the back of your right heel at your opponent by continuing the circular action of your right leg until it reaches the target. The right arm directed to the rear, and the left hand close to the body, are similar to the hand positions in the Back Thrusting Kick, which will not, unlike some others, interfere with the naturalness of the kicking action. (Photo 26).

NOTES

1. What was pointed out in Note 1 of the Back Thrust Kick is equally valid in the case of Ushiro-Mawashi-Geri. Initiation and performance of each phase of the kick must be done at high speed, otherwise it is quite a simple matter for the opponent to retreat out of range.

2. Also as in the case of the Back Thrust Kick you must avoid turning the right side of the body too far wards your opponent when doing the kick. This reduces the speed with which the kick can be applied. It also causes you to turn the right leg so that the top instead of the side of the leg is facing up when doing the kick. This position forces you to use the comparatively weak striking surface of the outside of the right foot instead of the correct and very solid striking surface of the back of the right heel. It also restricts the circling action of the kick, from which it derives its power. To avoid these mistakes therefore concentrate on keeping the side and not the front of the kicking leg facing up when doing the kick.

Ushiro-Mawashi-Geri

Yoko-Geri-Kekomi

INTRODUCTION

'Yoko' means 'side', 'geri' means 'kick', 'kekomi' means 'thrust'. When this kick is applied the side of the body is facing the target and the leg is used in a thrusting fashion. In the Front Kick the front of the body faces the opponent; in the Roundhouse Kick the front of the body is turned towards the opponent at an angle of about forty-five degrees; in the Back Kick the back is turned towards the opponent. With the Side Thrust Kick, the body is side-on to the opponent and therefore with its inclusion in our karate repertoire we possess kicking techniques which will enable us to make an attack irrespective of how the body turn to the opponent. This enables us to adhere to the karate principle of being able to handle any situation.

Things are not so simple in karate free-fighting, because you must be able to initiate the attacks from the free-fighting stance. You do not stand sideways waiting for an opportunity to do Side Thrust Kick. What you must do is position the body rapidly from the free-fighting stance as soon as you decide to attack. You must practice in a way which will enable you to execute any technique from the free-fighting stance by adapting your stance to the technique which you intend to use. The difficulty with the Side Kick is to change from the free-fighting stance to the sideways-on position rapidly and smoothly enough to do the Side Kick before the opponent has time to retreat out of range. With practice this difficulty can be overcome, but it seems that the people who excel in side-kicking are those with slim and supple hips. Although every karate player should be able to do Yoko-Geri-Kekomi, it is not the kind of kick that you should specialise in unless you are of a slim build.

This of course is not easy advice to follow, as side-kicking has certain very obvious advantages. The main one is that it can be done with a lot of power, and the position of the foot is such that the risk of bruising the foot against the opponent's anatomy is minimal. It also enables one to continue an attack after an opponent has avoided oi-zuki by jumping away to his left side. The Side Thrust Kick is also used as a 'stopper' when done with the foot which is kept in front in the free fighting stance. In this case you simply thrust the leg out to stop the opponent in his tracks, to nullify his attack and very often score a consequent point.

We see that though Yoko-geri-kekomi is not as useful in positive attack as Front Kick, Roundhouse Kick or the Back Kick, you should not neglect it but practice it so that it will enhance your proficiency in all-round karate free-fighting.

TECHNICAL DESCRIPTION

Assume the stance in Photo 1. Preserving your hand position, pivot anti-clockwise on the ball of your left foot and thrust your bent right leg forward and up with the leg turned slightly to your left. (Photo 27). Without pausing aim the edge of your right foot at your opponent by forcefully straightening your right leg in his direction, simultaneously twisting your right leg anti-clockwise and allowing your torso to turn sideways on to the opponent by continuing to pivot on the ball of your left foot. The right arm is straightened towards the opponent and the left fist drawn back to the left hip as you kick. More naturalness and freedom comes from this particular hand positioning. (Photo 28).

NOTES

1. Once more speed and determination are required to avoid giving the opponent time to retreat.

YOKO-GERI-KEKOMI WITH FOOT IN FRONT

As with Mawashi-Geri with the foot in front, unless you have long legs it is necessary to step into range and this is done with the right foot moving past the left and slightly out to your right. (Photo 29).

From here the technique is the same as with the rear foot, adapting the action to the other side, the left. Full instructions are given above. (Photo 30).

3 Shotokan karate

Yoko-Geri-Kekomi

YOKO-GERI-KEKOMI AS A "STOPPER"

This kick is used more than any other as a stopper. Assume the stance of Photo 1. Your opponent begins an oi-zuki attack. Push your left leg into the air, turning it slightly to your right. (Photo 31). Aim it at your opponent's mid-section, using the edge of the foot, and straighten the leg towards him as you simultaneously twist it clockwise, allowing your torso to turn sideways on to the opponent by pivoting on the ball of your right foot. Hand positions remain unchanged throughout. (Photo 32).

NOTES
1. Photo 32 shows a common alternative to the classical hand position shown in Photo 30. It is used mostly for Yoko-Geri-Kekomi when this kick is employed as a stopper. This is because the speed of a stopper does not always permit a change of hand position.
2. Notes 1 and 2 on "Mae-Geri-Kekomi" used as a stopper are equally valid here and should be read again and applied to "Yoko-Geri-Kekomi".

Tobi-Mae-Geri

INTRODUCTION

'Tobi' means 'jumping' and we are familiar with 'mae' and 'geri'. In doing this kick we jump into the air in order to do an airborne front kick. If you practice the ordinary front kicks frequently in free-fighting training you will be able without too much difficulty to carry out the Jumping Front Kick. The practice of the ordinary Front Kick will develop power and skill with the legs in a frontal direction. It will also help you to develop a sense of balance. In addition you will get used to the blocks and counters of your opponents to your front kick attacks. All these acquired skills will stand you in good stead when you begin jumping into the air to kick.

Once you feel confident when executing the ordinary front kicks, begin with an attempt at the Jumping Front Kick, at first without trying to rise too high in the air. Gradually, increase the height at which you do it, when engaged in free-fighting. Do not attempt it too frequently as this will take away the element of surprise essential to doing this technique in a way which will enable you to use it against your opponent before he has a chance to block or evade and counterattack before you can return to a strong defensive position with your feet firmly on the ground again.

If you do not heed this advice you will be deterred, as many karate players are, from using this kick, and never give yourself a chance to develop skill in its use. Trying it too often before you have skill and power in its use will mean that you will be constantly punished by your opponent before becoming earthbound again. In all techniques, but especially in kicks where one is balanced on only one leg or jumping into the air, one must accept that until a technique is done with naturalness, one's defensive alertness is temporarily distracted. An alert opponent will not be slow to take advantage of this. Therefore build gradually where this technique is concerned.

TECHNICAL DESCRIPTION

Assume stance of Photo 1. Spring into the air from your right foot and assist your rise by snapping the left foot into the air, then snap your right foot up past your left. (Photo 33). Continue to snap your right leg upwards, thrusting it towards your opponent, attempting at the same time to preserve a hand position which will enable you to adequately defend yourself should the need arise. (Photo 34).

Tobi-Yoko-Geri

35 36

INTRODUCTION

"Tobi' means 'jumping', 'yoko' means 'side', and 'geri' means 'kick'. In this technique we jump into the air in order to do a Side Kick.

What has been said about the Jumping Front Kick from the second paragraph to the end of the Introduction to Tobi-Mae-Geri is equally valid for the present technique.

TECHNICAL DESCRIPTION

Assume the stance of Photo 1. With a running action moving first your left foot diagonally forward to the left then moving your right foot in the same direction past your left foot, spring into the air from your right foot, while allowing your left leg to assist your rise upwards by bringing it up, then allowing your right leg, knee bent, to overtake it. (Photo 35).

By straightening your right leg, aim the side of your right foot at your opponent while allowing your left foot, sole up, to snap to a point on the lower point of your right thigh. Your right arm should be straight and pointing towards your opponent and your left fist should be withdrawn to your left hip. (Photo 36).

NOTE

When moving into position for the kick, care should be taken to avoid any attacking technique which the opponent may attempt to use, i.e. such as the punch shown in photos 35 and 36.

CHAPTER 2

Pure Defence Principle

THE PURE DEFENCE PRINCIPLE

Attack is the best form of defence, but sometimes the opponent delivers his attack before you do... You must also be able to defend yourself. This is an essential Karate skill. We have chosen some blocking and evasion techniques used by all karate free-fighting experts, to ensure you do not waste your time studying ineffective methods.

Gedan-Barai

GEDAN BARAI - INTRODUCTION

'Gedan' means 'downward' or 'lower level' and 'barai' means 'sweep'. Though 'gedan-barai' is used more often than the alternative term 'gedan-uke', the accepted English equivalent term 'downward block' is really a translation of 'gedan-uke'. For this technique we make a downward, sweeping action with the forearm, and, using the lower part of the little finger side of the forearm, block the opponent's attacking leg or arm. It is essential for effective 'jiyu-kumite' to be proficient in this block. Without it one's ability to defend against low kicking attacks especially is drastically reduced. 'Gedan-bari' is largely used for this purpose and is an effective defence against low-level attack.

TECHNICAL DESCRIPTION

Assume the stance of Photo 1 of this chapter. Your opponent attacks with Right Front Thrust Kick. Keeping your left fist strongly clenched, begin the block by straightening your left forearm forcefully downwards and at the same time starting to rotate your left arm clockwise. (Photo 2).

Continue to straighten and rotate your left arm, swing it powerfully out to your left, and with the lower part of the little finger side of the forearm just above the wrist bone, make strong contact with the lower part of the opponent's leg and force it out to your left, away from your body. Simultaneously twist your body to your right and withdraw your right fist to your right hip. (Photo 3).

Age-Uke

INTRODUCTION

'Age' means 'rising' and 'uke' means 'block'. When performing this technique we raise the forearm, and using the lower part of the little finger side of the forearm, block the opponent's attacking arm or leg when directed at face level. The full title of the technique is 'jodan-age-uke': 'jodan' means 'upper level'. The full meaning is 'upper level rising block'.

Age-uke is at its most effective when used against attacks that come straight at you from the front, as opposed to attacks which arrive in a circular or hooking fashion, such as Roundhouse Kicks, etc. Many attacks are made from the front so it can be easily appreciated how necessary it is to be able to do Age-Uke well.

4

TECHNICAL DESCRIPTION

Assume the stance of Photo 1, Chapter 2. Your opponent attempts a Right Lunge Punch to your face. Keeping your left fist firmly clenched, rotate your left forearm clockwise forcefully straight upwards, and with the little finger side of the forearm, just above the wrist bones, make strong contact with the lower part of your opponent's punching arm and force it up, thereby halting the progress of the punch towards you. Your body is twisted to your right and your right fist is withdrawn to your right hip. (Photo 4).

Soto-Ude-Uke

INTRODUCTION

'Soto' means 'outer', 'ude' means 'forearm', and as we know 'uke' means 'block'. In applying this techique we swing the forearm from the direction of the outer part of the body, away from the centre line, inwards towards the centre of the body, and, using the lower part of the little finger side of the forearm, block the opponent's attacking arm or leg.

Soto-Ude-Uke is one of the classical blocking techniques of karate and must be mastered by anyone wishing to excel in free-fighting. Though it is less important than Gedan-Barai or Age-Uke, as the position of the hands in the free-fighting stance lend themselves to an easier application of the latter techniques, it can be used on numerous occasions against chest and head level attacks. It is no use for low level attacks.

The benefits of learning it are desirable, but even so many people ignore it in free-fighting, due to the comparative complexity of learning it. This latter consideration should not deter you from studying it, with its resulting benefits for free-fighting.

TECHNICAL DESCRIPTION

Assume the first stance shown in this chapter. Your opponent lunges at you with a Right Oi-zuki to the solar plexus. Keep your fist firmly clenched, and rotating your left forearm anti-clockwise while at the same time increasing the bend in your left arm and swinging your left forearm forcefully in towards the centre of your body, with the little finger side of your left forearm just above the wrist bone make strong contact with the lower part of the opponent's punching arm and force it out to your right, deflecting his punch. Your body twists to your right and your right fist is withdrawn to your right hip. (Photo 5).

NOTES
1. In order to use the outer forearm block against a high attack, you simply raise the blocking arm higher.

Ude-Barai

INTRODUCTION

'Ude' means 'forearm' and 'barai' means 'sweep'. We make a sweeping action with the forearm across the body, using the thick part of the forearm on the same side as the back of the hand, to block the opponent's attacking arm or leg.

This is a very powerful block since a very powerful swinging action of the body can be placed behind it. It is most useful against medium or low attacks. It is not very useful against head attacks. A lot of practice is necessary to perfect it since it travels from the outer side of the body, in towards the centre, necessarily dropping the blocking arm low as a preparatory measure against low attacks. A lot of people neglect this block as it is difficult to perfect to the right speed. If you tend to hold the left hand rather low, as those who favour 'ude-barai' do, then there is no problem in preparing for it. If you need added power then move your left blocking arm out to your left before doing it. If you not only hold your hand low but also out to the left then there is no need to make any hand preparation whatever. Simply move the blocking arm across the body from its usual position, into the blocking action.

The best way to get used to doing 'ude-barai-' is to practice it from the different positions mentioned. Another way is to use it often after the Downward Block as the position of the arm after the Downward Block makes it simple to move smoothly into Ude Barai. This is why this sequence of blocks is used so much, which is another good reason for developing a strong and skilful Ude Barai.

TECHNICAL DESCRIPTION

Assume the stance in Photo 1 chapter 2. Your opponent makes a Right Lunge Punch to your solar plexus. Keep your left fist firmly clenched, and rotating your left forearm clockwise, simultaneously straighten your left arm and push it forcefully across your body to your right and with the thick part of the forearm on the same side as the back of the hand, make strong contact with the lower part of your opponent's punching arm and deflect the punch away from your body to your right. Twist your body to your right and withdraw your right fist to your right hip. (Photo 6).

Te-Nagashi-Uke

7

INTRODUCTION

'Te' means 'hand'. 'Nagashi', like 'barai' is translated best by the word 'sweep'. 'Uke' means 'block'. The name of this technique refers to the fact that when applying it we block the attacking arm or leg by sweeping it to one side with the palm of the hand. The **'Te-nagashi-uke'** is a very useful and interesting block which all Jiyu-Kumite players should be able to do. But, since it is done with the hand open, injury to the fingers can happen if it is not done with skill. Before using it against kicking attacks, build up skill in its application by using it first against arm attacks. No matter how skilful you become in this technique, always use great care when using it to avert injury to the fingers.

TECHNICAL DESCRIPTION

Assume the stance in Photo 1 chapter 2, the free-fighting stance. Your opponent attempts a Left Side Thrust Kick. Rotating your left arm clockwise, straighten and lower it, and opening the left hand so that the fingers are firm and straight and in line with the palm, and the thumb is tucked in so as to avoid hurting it make strong contact with your left palm with the lower part of the back of the opponent's kicking leg, and push it forcefully with a sweeping action to your left, away from your body. Your body twists to your right and your right fist is withdrawn to your right hip. (Photo 7).

Gedan-Kake-Uke

INTRODUCTION

As we know, 'gedan' means 'downward'. 'Kake' means 'hooking' and 'uke' means 'block'. The name of this technique refers to the fact that we swing the arm downward and block the opponent's kick by hooking his leg near the heel with that part of the wrist just above the thumb and forcing his foot off target. This block can be executed from left to right or vice-versa. The former method is more widely used. At first this blocking technique will not impress you as being of much practical value, but if you persevere you will find that it can be built up into a precise and powerful blocking weapon against low or fairly low kicking techniques. Gedan-Kake-Uke, however, has no value as a method of defence against techniques done with the upper limbs.

TECHNICAL DESCRIPTION - LEFT TO RIGHT

Assume the Jiyu-Kumite stance. Your opponent tries a Right Front Thrust Kick.

Keep your left fist firmly clenched, and lowering and straightening your left arm twist it slightly to your right, and with that part of your forearm on the same side as the thumb, a couple of inches up the wrist, hook the lower part of the back and outside of the opponent's kicking leg, forcing it away from your body to your right and at the same time upwards while gradually bending your left arm. This hooking action enables you not only to render the opponent's kick ineffective but enables you to trap his leg with your arm, giving you a strong advantage. Your body is twisted to your right and your right fist is withdrawn to your right hip. (Photo 8).

TECHNICAL DESCRIPTION - RIGHT TO LEFT

In the same stance your opponent attempts a Right Front Thrust Kick. Keeping your left fist firmly clenched lower and straighten your left arm. (Photo 9).

Using the thumb side of the left forearm a couple of inches above the wrist, hook the lower part of the back and inside of the opponent's kicking leg and force it away from your body to your left and at the same time upwards, gradually bending your left arm. In this case also the back hooking action of the block enables you to trap the leg with your arm. In this block the body is twisted to your left, not right, as the mechanics of this technique are such that a twist to the left best enables you to achieve maximum power. (Photo 10).

Sukui-Uke

INTRODUCTION

'Sukui' means 'scooping' and 'uke' means 'block'. In applying this technique we scoop with a cupped hand the ankle of the opponent and pull his leg forward and upward, rendering his kick ineffective. As in the case of the downward hooking block, this block is no use against punching and striking techniques. It is best employed against low kicks, especially those which come straight at you, as distinct from those which come in a curve, e.g. mawashi-geri. When you are adept at this block you can use it against such kicks too. It can be used by cupping the hand to right or left.

A caution must be given since it is an open-hand block to exert great care when applying Sukui-Uke so at all costs to avoid injury to the fingers by making violent contact with them against a kicking leg or foot.

TECHNICAL - HAND CUPPED TO RIGHT

Assume the stance in Photo 1 chapter 2. Attack is made by your opponent with a Right Front Thrust Kick. Straighten and drop your left arm just outside the kicking leg, left hand cupped to right. Scoop the ankle from underneath and pull his leg forward and upward. Not only do you effectively stop the kick but you radically upset your opponent's balance, and thereby gain an advantage over him. Your body is twisted to your right and your right fist is withdrawn to your right hip. (Photo 11).

TECHNICAL - HAND CUPPED TO LEFT

From the Free-Fighting Stance your opponent tries a low Left Front Thrust Kick. Straighten and drop your left hand just outside the opponent's leg; rotate your left hand clockwise and with the hand cupped to your left, scoop his ankle from underneath and pull his leg forward and upward. You thereby stop his kick and and disturb his balance. Your body is twisted to your right and your right fist is withdrawn to your right hip. (Photo 12).

Tsukamai-Uke

INTRODUCTION

'Tsukamai' means 'grasping' and 'uke' means 'block'. We block the opponent's attack by grasping his sleeve, thereby being able to control his arm and take useful advantage of this. Tsukamai-Uke can be used effectively against punching or striking techniques, but is rarely used against kicks. Your skill in this block will reveal to you its versatility. It can be used from all kinds of direction, whilst positioning the hand which grasps in various ways. This block provides you with food for thought. Remember the care which must be exercised when employing a technique using the open hand, where the risk of injuring the fingers is involved.

TECHNICAL DESCRIPTION

Assume the stance in Photo 1 chapter 2. Your opponent tries a Right Lunge Punch to the face. Before the punch gets too close, open your left hand and with the fingers pointing up, slap it forcefully against the lower part of the little finger side of the opponent's right forearm. Then quickly grasp his sleeve on the same side of his arm by firmly closing your left hand over the cloth of the sleeve and push his arm so that the force of the punch is diverted to your right. To divert the punch is not the only result of this block. It also enables you to control the opponent's movement to a certain extent, giving you an advantage. Your body is twisted to your right and your right fist drawn to your right hip. (Photo 13).

NOTES.

1. If he attempts a low punch you should point the fingers of the grasping hand downwards for the slap, prior to actually grasping his sleeve. Against this kind of punch you can also apply Tsukamai-Uke by grasping the sleeve on the top of the punching arm, inside the punching arm or under the punching arm, exerting force in different directions.

If you grasp the sleeve on top, the back of the grasping hand should be facing up and the fingers pointing to your right. Grasping inside, the back of the grasping hand should be facing to your right and the fingers pointing to the ground when you slap. Grasping under the back of the hand should be facing the ground and the fingers pointing to your right when you slap, prior to grasping the sleeve.

Jodan-Shuto-Uke

INTRODUCTION

'Jodan' means 'upper level'. The first syllable for 'shuto', 'shu', means, like 'te', 'hand'. The second syllable, 'to', means 'knife'. 'Shuto' means therefore 'knife-hand'. The side of the hand from the bottom of the wrist to the end of the little finger is used like a knife: in a slashing and not a stabbing manner. The word 'uke' means 'block'. The whole term 'jodan-shuto-uke' means that we use the side of the hand to block a high attack.

This technique can also be used against attacks to the chest area, when it is known as 'chudan-shuto-uke', 'chudan' meaning 'mid-level'. Attacks which come lower than this are blocked by 'gedan-shuto-uke', 'gedan' meaning 'lower level'. Blocks seem to be most useful using this technique at the upper level, less useful at mid-level and inclined to result in injury to the fingers when used against a kicking attack to the lower level. We have therefore chosen 'jodan-shuto-uke' to illustrate the use of this technique. Care must be exercised when using this open-hand block.

TECHNICAL DESCRIPTION

Assume the stance of Jiyu-Kumite. Your opponent attempts a Right Lunge Punch to your face. Moving your weight backwards towards your right leg, open your left hand, and bending the hand backwards, forcefully rotate it clockwise up and to your left while straightening the left arm and using the side of the hand between the little finger and the wrist, strike the inside of the lower part of the forearm of the opponent's punching hand. Your body is twisted to your right and your open right hand with thumb tucked in and fingers pointed is withdrawn to a position covering your solar plexus. The effect of this technique is to divert the force of the opponent's punch away from you to your left.

NOTES

1. We have shown here the classical way of doing this technique, the weight of the body is moved backwards on to the right leg and the right hand taken to the solar plexus. We cannot always assume this stance; often one must use this block from the free-fighting stance. An alternative move for the right hand is to withdraw the hand to the right hip. One can also use this variation in the classical stance.

Haiwan-Nagashi-Uke

INTRODUCTION

"Hai' means 'back', 'wan' means 'arm', 'nagashi' as we know means 'sweeping' and 'uke' means 'block'. The name of this technique reveals the fact that we block the opponent's attack with a sweeping sort of action using the back of the forearm - that part of the forearm on the same side as the back of the hand.

This block is only used against high attacks.

TECHNICAL DESCRIPTION

Assume the stance of photo 1 chapter 2. Your opponent attempts a Right Lunge Punch to your face. Rotating the left forearm clockwise push it upwards and out to your left, and with the thick part of the forearm on the same side as the back of the hand, strike the inside of the lower part of the opponent's punching arm, diverting the force of the punch away from your body to your left. Your body is twisted to your right and your right fist is withdrawn to your right hip. (Photo 15).

Otoshi-Uke

INTRODUCTION

'Otoshi' means 'dropping'. Here we block the arm or leg attacking by dropping the forearm on to it. As this block occurs seldom in Jiyu-Kumite it is not as valuable to you as the previously described blocks. The one situation where this block may be used to very good effect is as follows.

TECHNICAL DESCRIPTION

Assume the stance for Free-Style. Your opponent attempts a Right Front Snap Kick. In other words his attack is coming upwards towards you. Rapidly bringing your left arm closer to your body and across to your right while bending your arm more at the elbow, rotate your left forearm clockwise and drop the thick part of the little-finger side of your left forearm forcefully down on top of the shin of the opponent's kicking leg, effectively blocking the kick before it reaches you. At the same time increase the force of the block by pushing your body weight downwards in the direction of the block. Do not in this case turn your body to your right, as this would only detract from the direct downward force to your front required in this particular blocking technique. Your right fist as usual is withdrawn to your right hip. See Photo 16.

Yokeru-Koto

INTRODUCTION

'Yokeru' is a Japanese verb which means 'evade'. The way a verb is turned into a noun in Japanese is simply to put the word 'koto' - 'things' - on to the end of the verb. 'Yokeru-koto' means 'evasions', which is the noun from the verb 'evade'.

In karate free-fighting one must become profoundly accustomed to employing two types of defensive action. The most important is blocking, which we have just covered. Not as important, but still important, especially in the case of people who are not particularly heavy or strong, is that type of defensive action we call 'evasions' - 'yokeru-koto' - dealt with next.

Unlike blocking techniques, the evasion techniques consist simply in moving one's body in such a way that the opponent's techniques can be avoided. The ideal way to defend against an attack is to evade and at the same time block. Any blocking technique will do. After learning the following ways of evading an attack, you should make it positively your business to become skilful in using them in combination with the blocking techniques.

Do not forget though that your opponent's attack will be so quick that you may not always evade it. You will then be completely depending on your ability to block his attack. This situation is a true test of your blocking ability.

If you really practice the following evasion movements with intelligence and courage you will find that your skill in this type of defensive action becomes such that frequently you will be able to evade your opponents' attack without having to resort to blocks. In free-fighting the most commonly used evasions are three. Concentrate on these and also practice your karate attacking and blocking regularly and seriously until you find that your body will also do the little subtle variations of these main evasive movements quite naturally. By means of studying these three main basic evasions, you will not only develop the fine sense of timing necessary to bring off an evasion but will also become more and more aware of the nature of evasion. This sense of timing and experience will then enable you to act in a creative manner and evolve other forms of evasions which you can use to handle situations less classical than those which can be handled by the three main forms.

Ushiro-Ni-Yokeru-Koto

INTRODUCTION

'Ushiro ni' means literally 'to the rear'. 'Ushiro' means 'rear' and 'ni' means 'to'.

The 'ushiro-ni-yokeru-koto' is the most widely used of the evasion moves because all that is required is to retreat out of range. All that is involved is putting oneself out of range to the exclusion of other techniques such as blocking, countering, getting into a position of advantage and so on.

TECHNICAL DESCRIPTION

Jiyu-kumite stance. Your opponent attempts Right Lunge Punch. Retreat out of range by first moving the right foot out of its present position, to the rear. (Photo 17). As soon as the right foot is firmly in place shift your weight back and draw back the left foot. (photo 18). Thus you are effectively out of range.

Hidari-Naname-Ni-Yokeru-Koto

INTRODUCTION

'Hidari' means 'left', 'naname-ni' means 'diagonal', and 'yokeru-koto' means 'evasion'.

This method of evasion is more difficult than the retreating method because a greater degree of precision is required in the timing, and the mechanics of the diagonal evasions are more complicated. Why, one might ask, spend time on a more complicated and difficult evasion when we already have a simpler? The answer lies in the fact that when we evade in a diagonal direction the attacker is still travelling in the direction of attack, and is thereby at a disadvantage before he can recover and re-align himself with your new position. Thus a counter-attack at that moment would really test his ability to block or otherwise defend himself. This type of evasion if combined in jiyu-kumite with the retreating directly backwards method enables you to confuse your opponent. This is a very important factor in doing free-fighting well.

TECHNICAL DESCRIPTION

Assume the free-fighting stance. Your opponent tries a Right Lunge Punch. Evade by first moving your left foot diagonally to your left rear.(Photo 19). Without pausing move your right foot diagonally to your left front, finishing up facing your opponent in the southpaw free-fighting stance. (Photo 20). As can be seen, these movements lead to an effective evasion of the opponent's attack.

NOTES

1. When evading in this way it is essential to wait until the attacker is almost on top of you before you move. Otherwise, your opponent will see your intention before he has committed himself, and will be able to re-adjust his position and quickly deliver a new attack in the appropriate direction.

Migi-Naname-Ni-Yokeru-Koto

INTRODUCTION

"Migi' means 'right', and as we know, 'naname-ni' means 'diagonal' and 'yokeru-koto' means 'evasion'.

This method of evasion is less popular than the Left Diagonal Evasion because the latter evasion makes it possible for you to put a greater distance between you and your opponent, using as it does the leading left leg, not the rear leg, in the initial movement. Regarding the function of the Right Diagonal Evasion, the last two paragraphs of the previous technique in the introductory section apply equally to it.

TECHNICAL DESCRIPTION

Assume the free-fighting stance. Your opponent attempts a Right Lunge Punch. Evade by moving your right foot then your left diagonally to your right rear, finishing up facing your opponent in the orthodox free-fighting stance. (photo 21). As can be seen, these movements enable you to effectively evade to your right.

NOTES
See previous notes which are equally applicable.

CHAPTER 3

THE CONTINUATION— ATTACK PRINCIPLE

INTRODUCTION

As we have seen in chapter two that by training it is possible for a karate man to become skilful in blocking and evading his opponent's attacks, the next logical step is to become skilled in delivering what are called continuation attacks. This is to deliver another attacking technique after one's first technique has been nullified in some way by one's opponent.

Theoretically one could carry on attacking after each attack, ad infinitum, making a new attack after each block. But by tacit agreement continuous attacking involves only two or three techniques to prevent a karate contest becoming rough and uncontrolled. We shall therefore limit the continuous attacking principle sequences to two techniques.

We shall be using mainly techniques which we have already introduced in previous chapters. The new ones are: 'yoko-kentsui-uchi(side fist hammer strike) which is used as the second technique in the second combination in this chapter: Right Oi-zuki and Right Yoko-Kentsui-Uchi.

The second new technique is 'shuto-uchi'(knife hand strike), which is used as the second technique in the eighth combination of techniques in this chapter: Left Yoko Geri and Right Shuto-Uchi.

The third exception is 'yoko-ura-ken-uchi(side back-fist strike), which is used as the second technique in the final combination of techniques in this chapter: Right Ushiro Geri and Right Yoko-Ura-Ken-Uchi.

The reason why these techniques have not been introduced earlier is that they are not primarily ones which are used to initiate an attack but as follow-up techniques when an initial attack has failed and you finish up rather close to your opponent.

Right Oi-Zuki & Left Gyaku-Zuki

TECHNICAL DESCRIPTION

Face your opponent in the free-fighting stance, photo 1 on this page. Your high Right Lunge Punch is blocked by your opponent with Left Rising Block. (Photo 2). You are close to your opponent; his left hand is high in the air leaving his mid-section momentarily unguarded; swiftly continue your attack with a powerful left reverse punch to the solar plexus. (Photo 3).

Right Oi-Zuki & Right Yoko-Kentsui-Uchi

INTRODUCTION

'Yoko' means 'side', 'ken' means 'fist', 'tsui' means 'hammer' and 'uchi' means 'strike'. We strike to the side using the muscular part of the little finger side of the fist, firmly clenched; which part is likened to a hammer. The hammershaft is the forearm.

TECHNICAL DESCRIPTION

Assume the free-fighting stance. Your opponent dodges your Right Lunge Punch by making a rather short Left Diagonal evasion. The assumption is that he has not had time to put much distance in between you and himself by his evasion. (Photo 4).

As your opponent is positioned at your right side and also rather close to you, you continue with a Right Side Fist Hammer Strike. Get ready by swinging your right fist across the upper part of the chest to the left keeping the back of the fist facing up. To counterbalance this strong action of the right arm and fist you thrust your left fist, palm down, under your armpit. As you prepare your hands in this way, start moving your right foot even closer to the opponent. (Photo 5).

Then apply the strike by twisting your body more to the right, swinging your right fist horizontally in an arc to your right side and aiming the little finger side of the clenched fist, back facing up, at an upper part of your opponent's anatomy. Simultaneously you complete your stepping action with the right foot towards your opponent and withdraw your left fist to your left hip. (Photo 6).

Right Oi-Zuki & Right Mawashi-Geri

TECHNICAL DESCRIPTION

Face your opponent in the free-fighting stance. Your opponent dodges your Right Lunge Punch by making a rather longer Left Diagonal Evasion than he made in the previous technical article. (Photo 7).

If the opponent has moved so far from you that he cannot be reached with an arm technique, such as the Side Fist Hammer Strike used in the previous Continuation Attack Combination, then the leg, having greater reach, can be used instead. The best one in this case is the Right Roundhouse Kick. Swiftly bring your left foot nearer to your opponent to get within range, and execute this kicking technique. (Photo 8).

NOTES

1. If you have long legs, or if the distance separating you from the opponent is not too great after he has made his Left Diagonal Evasion, then there is no need to move the left foot nearer before applying the technique; you can simply do the kick by keeping the left foot where it is after you have done the Right Lunge Punch.

TECHNICAL DESCRIPTION OF THE PREVIOUS METHOD IN DIFFERENT CIRCUMSTANCES.

Face your opponent in Jiyu-Kumite stance. Your opponent puts himself out of range of your Right Lunge Punch by making a Retreating Evasion. (Photo 9).

To continue your attack with advantage, simply allow your left foot to slide forward swiftly and naturally towards your right foot in order to get within range for the attack and then apply a Right Roundhouse Kick. (Photo 10).

Right Mae-Geri-Kekomi & Right Oi-Zuki

TECHNICAL DESCRIPTION

Face your opponent in the free-fighting stance. Your opponent blocks your low Right Front Thrust Kick with, for example, a Downward Block. (Photo 11). The fact that you are now close to your opponent and that his left arm is in a low position, leaving his face unguarded, enables you to continue your attack with advantage by swiftly putting your right foot to the ground and delivering a high Right Lunge Punch. (Photo 12).

Left Mawashi-Geri & Right Gyaku-Zuki

TECHNICAL DESCRIPTION

Face your opponent in the free-fighting stance. Your opponent blocks your low Left Roundhouse Kick, with, for example, Right Downward Block. (Photo 13). You are rather close to your opponent and his face is unguarded, enabling you to continue with your attack by swiftly getting your left foot to the ground and by applying a high Right Reverse Punch. (Photo 14).

Left Yoko-Geri-Kekomi & Right Ushiro-Mawashi-Geri

TECHNICAL DESCRIPTION

Face your opponent, each of you in the free-fighting stance. Your opponent deflects your Left Side Thrust Kick, with for example a Left Hand-Sweeping Block. (Photo 15). From your position shown in Photo 15, it is quite easy to continue your attack with advantage by simply placing your left foot swiftly to the ground in front of your opponent's left foot and pointing in the same direction, and turning your back to the opponent, execute a high Right Back Roundhouse Kick. (Photo 16).

Left Yoko-Geri-Kekomi & Right Shuto-Uchi

INTRODUCTION

As was explained in the introduction to the block, "Jodan-Shuto-Uke", the first syllable of "Shuto", "Shu", means "Hand", and the second syllable, "To", means "Knife". The word "Shuto" means therefore, "Knife Hand", and refers to the fact that the side of the hand between the bottom of the wrist and the little finger is used like a knife, and in a slashing not a stabbing manner. As we already know, "Uchi" means "Strike". The term "Shuto-Uchi", therefore, refers to the fact that when we apply this technique we use the side of the hand for the purpose of striking.

TECHNICAL DESCRIPTION

Face your opponent in the free-fighting stance. Your opponent deflects your left side thrust kick, using for example a left hand sweeping block. (Photo 17). You can then continue your attack with a Right Knife-Hand Block. Do this by turning your back to your opponent by swiftly placing your left foot to the left side of him and with your left foot pointing approximately in the same direction as his. At the same time open your right hand completely, fingers firm and pointed, close together, and palm facing downwards swing it across your chest, pulling your left fist to your left hip, and glance over your right shoulder. (Photo 18).

Without breaking your turning momentum bring your right foot towards your opponent, and with your right side towards him, aim the side of your right hand at the side of the opponent's upper level target area by swinging, straightening and fully extending your arm in his direction. (Photo 19).

17

18

19

Right Ushiro-Geri-Kekomi & Right Yoko-Ura-Ken-Uchi

INTRODUCTION

'Yoko' means 'side', 'ken' means 'fist, and 'uchi' means 'strike'. 'Ura' simply means 'back.' In applying this technique we strike to our side, using the back of the fist when the fist is firmly clenched.

TECHNICAL DESCRIPTION

Assume the free-fighting stance. Your opponent blocks your Right Back Thrust Kick, using, for example, a Forearm Sweep. (Photo 20).

After your kick has been blocked, you can with advantage continue your attack with a Right Yoko-Ura-Ken-Uchi. So quickly swinging your right clenched fist with the back facing up across your chest and turning your body to your right, face your opponent with your right foot placed to the ground close to the inside of his left foot and aim the back of your right clenched fist at the side of the opponent's face. This is done by swinging, straightening, and fully extending your right arm towards him while simultaneously rotating it clockwise. Your left fist remains, throughout the technique, fixed to your left hip. (Photo 21).

20

21

CHAPTER 4

THE CONTINUATION— DEFENCE PRINCIPLE

INTRODUCTION

As we saw in Chapter Three, it is possible by intelligent, systematic training for a karate man to become skilful in delivering with speed and power a second technique after his first one has been defended against. The next logical step in one's karate training is to train with the object of developing skill in defending oneself against an opponent who is expert in delivering another technique as soon as his first has been thwarted.

This chapter will be concerned with the principle of continuation blocking or defence, involving the use of one block or defensive measure straight after another.

NOTE: We shall be using in this chapter only techniques which have already been introduced.

There is one exception which is 'morote-tate-ude-uke'. This means 'two-handed perpendicular forearm block'. It will be introduced in full when it appears; it is not a very common block as the opportunity for using it does not occur very often.

Left Age-Uke & Left Tsukamai-Uke

TECHNICAL DESCRIPTION

Face your opponent, each of you in the free-fighting stance. (Photo 1). Assume you have blocked your opponent's high Right Lunge Punch with a Left Rising Block. (Photo 2). If your opponent then continues his attack with a Left Reverse Punch to your solar plexus, you can nullify this second attack by simply dropping your left hand forcefully down from its present position and applying a Left Grasping Block against the top of the sleeve of the opponent's punching arm. (Photo 3).

NOTE: This is the first time that this variation of Tsukamai-Uke has been actually illustrated, but it was mentioned in the note to the article on Tsukamai-Uke in Chapter Two.

Hidari-Naname-Ni-Yokeru-Koto & Right Haiwan-Nagashi-Uke

TECHNICAL DESCRIPTION

Assume the free-fighting stance. Your opponent has just delivered a high Right Lunge Punch which you have dodged using a short Left Diagonal Evasion. (Photo 4). If he then continues his attack with a Right Side Fist-Hammer Strike to the right side of your head, you can nullify this second attack effectively by applying a Right Back-Arm Sweeping Block against the lower part of the little finger side of the opponent's striking arm. (Photo 5).

Hidari-Naname-Ni-Yokeru-Koto & Right Ude-Barai

TECHNICAL DESCRIPTION

Face your opponent, each in the free-fighting stance. Assume you have dodged your opponent's high Right Lunge Punch by making a rather long Left Diagonal Evasion. (Photo 6). If the opponent continues his attack with a Right Roundhouse kick to your stomach, you can nullify this second attack by applying a right forearm sweep against the front of the opponent's right shin. (Photo 7).

Ushiro-Ni-Yokeru-Koto & Left Gedan-Barai

TECHNICAL DESCRIPTION

Assume the free-fighting stance. You have put yourself out of range of the opponent's Right Lunge Punch by making a Retreating Evasion. (Photo 8). If the opponent then continues his attack with a Right Roundhouse Kick to your stomach, you can nullify this by applying a Left Downward Block against the front of the opponent's right shin. (Photo 9).

Left Gedan-Barai & Left Age-Uke

TECHNICAL DESCRIPTION

Face your opponent, each of you in the free-fighting stance. Assume you have blocked your opponent's low Right Front Thrust Kick with a Left Downward Block. (Photo 10). If the opponent then continues his attack with a Right Lunge Punch to your face you can nullify this second attack by quickly swinging your left arm upwards from its present position and applying a Left Rising Block against your opponent's punching arm. (Photo 11).

Right Gedan-Barai & Right Soto-Ude-Uke

TECHNICAL DESCRIPTION

From the free-fighting stance assume you have blocked your opponent's low Left Roundhouse Kick with a Right Downward Block. (Photo 12). If the opponent then continues his attack with a Right Reverse Punch to your face, you can nullify this second attack by swinging your right arm from its present position upwards and across your body and applying a Right Outer Forearm Block against your opponent's punching arm. (Photo 13). Although this is the first time this high kind of Soto-Ude-Uke has actually been illustrated, it was mentioned in the article on Soto-Ude-Uke in chapter two.

Left Te-Nagashi-Uke & Right Gedan-Barai

TECHNICAL DESCRIPTION

From the free-fighting stance you have deflected your opponent's low Left Side Thrust Kick with a Left Hand-Sweeping Block. (Photo 14). If your opponent continues his attack with a Right Back Roundhouse kick to your stomach you can nullify this second attack by twisting your body to your left and applying a Right Downward Block against the back of your opponent's kicking leg. (Photo 15).

Left Te Nagashi-Uke & Left Tsukami-Uke

TECHNICAL DESCRIPTION

From the free-fighting stance assume you have deflected your opponent's low Left Side Thrust Kick with a Left Hand-Sweeping Block. (Photo 16).

If your opponent continues to attack with a Right Knife-Hand Strike to the right side of your neck you can nullify this second attack by swinging your left arm from its present position up and across your body and apply a Left Grasping Block against your opponent's striking arm. (Photo 17).

Left Ude-Barai & Morote-Tate-Ude-Uke

INTRODUCTION

'Morote' means 'two-handed' and 'tate' means 'perpendicular'. 'Ude' means 'forearm' and 'uke' means 'block' as we already know. The name indicates that we use both forearms pointing upwards to block the opponent's attack.

TECHNICAL DESCRIPTION

Face your opponent, each in the free-fighting stance. Assume you have blocked your opponent's Right Back Thrust Kick with a Left Forearm Sweep. (Photo 18). If your opponent then continues his attack with a Right Side Back-Fist Strike to the right side of your head, you can nullify this second attack by applying the Two-Handed Perpendicular Forearm Block. This is simply done by pointing both fists into the air, and with your forearms perpendicular, blocking the back of your opponent's striking arm with the little finger side of each arm. (Photo 19).

CHAPTER 5

THE BLOCK AND COUNTER-ATTACK PRINCIPLE

INTRODUCTION

In chapter four we demonstrated the principle of continuation defence with blocking techniques and evasive moves. Though this is absolutely necessary, it is even more important to be able to deliver a skilful counterattack. That is, to deliver it almost simultaneously with a blocking technique. In this way we can get in with an attacking technique before the opponent can follow his first technique with a second attacking technique.

Persevere in training to acquire this skill and you will eventually succeed.

The following block and counter techniques in the sequences shown are 'classical' and aptly illustrate the principle with which we are concerned in this chapter: do not be deterred because you find you do not have a great deal of success, at first.

NOTE: In this chapter we shall be using, with four exceptions, only techniques which have already been introduced in previous chapters. The first exception is 'Mawashi-zuki' - Roundhouse punch. The second exception is 'Mawashi-empi-uchi' - Roundhouse elbow strike; the third is 'Ura-zuki' - close punch; the fourth is 'Kagi-zuki' - Hook punch. These four will be formally introduced in their respective articles. They have been introduced here instead of earlier because they are not used as much as initiating-attack techniques but can be put to good use after blocking an attack and finishing up rather close to an opponent.

Left Age-Uke & Right Gyaku-Zuki

TECHNICAL DESCRIPTION

Face your opponent in the free-fighting stance. Assume you have blocked your opponent's high Right Lunge Punch with a Left Rising Block. (Photo 2). Your position now in relation to your opponent enables you to use with naturalness a Right Reverse Punch as your counter-attack. (Photo 3).

TECHNICAL DESCRIPTION

Face your opponent each of you in the free-fighting stance. Assume you have blocked your opponent's low Right Front Thrust Kick with a Left Downward Block. (Photo 4).

As in the previous article the most natural counter-attack to apply from your present position is a Right Reverse punch. (Photo 5).

Left Gedan-Barai Right Gyaku-Zuki

Right Haiwan-Nagashi-Uke & Right Shuto-Uchi

NOTE:
TECHNICAL DESCRIPTION
In the eight combination techniques in chapter three, we showed the Knife Hand Strike being applied from left to right, where the palm of the striking hand faces down. This technique can also be applied from right to left, in which case the palm of the striking hand faces up, which method of striking we shall describe in this article.

DESCRIPTION

Face your opponent in the free fighting stance. If you have blocked your opponent's high Left Roundhouse Kick with a Right Back-Arm Sweeping Block, (Photo 6), the right hand is conveniently placed for applying a Knife Hand Strike from right to left. Simply swing your right arm from right to left while rotating it clockwise and straightening it in the opponent's direction. Simultaneously, open the right hand with fingers firm and pointed and close together, and with the palm facing up, aim the right side of the hand at the left side of your opponent's upper level target area. (Photo 7).

Left Te-Nagashi-Uke & Left Mawashi-Geri

TECHNICAL DESCRIPTION

Face your opponent, each of you in the free-fighting stance. Assume you have blocked your opponent's low Left Side Thrust Kick. (Photo 8).

Your position now in relation to your opponent enables you quite naturallly to bring your right foot closer to your left and apply a Left Roundhouse Kick as your counter attack. (Photo 9).

NOTE

If you are near enough after doing the block to apply the kick without bringing your right foot closer to your left, then of course there is not need to make this stepping action.

Left Sukui-Uke & Right Mawashi-Zuki

INTRODUCTION

'Mawashi' means 'circular' or 'round' and 'zuki' means 'punch'. This technique has come to be known in English as the Roundhouse Punch. The name of the technique refers to the fact that in applying it we punch in a circular fashion.

10

TECHNICAL DESCRIPTION

From a free-fighting stance your opponent tries a low Left Side Thrust Kick which you block with a Left Scooping Block. (Photo 10). This kind of block enables you to pull your opponent very close to you and to your left. This position is ideal for the application of the Roundhouse Punch as your counter attack. Do this by simply aiming the front of your clenched right fist at the side of your opponent's face via a circular, anti-clockwise route, while at the same time rotating the right fist and arm anti-clockwise. Your right side is twisted in the direction of the punch and your left fist is withdrawn to your left hip. (Photo 11).

11

Left Ude-Barai & Right Mawashi-Empi-Uchi

12

13

INTRODUCTION

As you already know, 'mawashi' means 'circular' or 'round' and 'uchi' means 'strike'. 'Empi' means 'elbow'. This technique has come to be known in English as the Roundhouse Elbow Strike. The name of this technique refers to the fact that in applying it, we strike with the elbow via a circular route.

TECHNICAL DESCRIPTION

From the free-fighting stance you block your attacker's Right Back Thrust Kick with a Left Forearm Sweep. (Photo 12). When this happens the opponent will often finish up very close to you with the right side of his rib cage exposed. This position is ideal for the application of our counter. Do this by aiming the front of your right elbow at the right side of your opponent's rib cage via a circular, anti-clockwise route, while at the same time rotating the right arm anti-clockwise so that the back of the right fist finishes up facing upwards. Your right side is twisted in the direction of the punch and your left fist is withdrawn to your left hip. (Photo 13).

Left Ude-Barai & Right Ura-Zuki

INTRODUCTION

'Ura' in this case means 'close' and 'zuki' means 'punch'. The name signifies that it is a technique which is useful when close to the opponent.

TECHNICAL DESCRIPTION

From the free-fighting stance assume you have blocked your opponent's Right Back Thrust Kick with a Left Forearm Sweep. (Photo 14). When this happens, as we saw in the previous article, the opponent will often finish up close to you with his rib cage exposed. You can use the Close Punch as an alternative to the Roundhouse Elbow Strike. So, keeping the back of your right fist facing the ground, with a short, determined, thrusting action, aim the forefist straight at the right side of your opponent's rib cage while giving the fist a slight clockwise twist. Your right side is twisted in the direction of the punch and your left fist is withdrawn to your left hip. (Photo 15).

Left Tsukamai-Uke & Right Kagi-Zuki

INTRODUCTION

'Kagi' means 'hook' and 'zuki' means 'punch'. The name of this technique refers to that fact that in applying it we punch with the punching arm hook-shaped.

TECHNICAL DESCRIPTION

Assume the free-fighting stance and assume that you have blocked your opponent's high Right Lunge Punch with a Left Grasping Block. (Photo 16).

Your position is ideal for the use of Right Hook Punch. So, moving yourself closer and at right angles to the opponent by moving your left foot to his rear and pointing both feet to your front, aim your right forefist at your opponent's solar plexus as you rotate your right arm, hook shaped anti-clockwise, so that you complete the punch with the back of the right fist facing upwards. Your left fist is withdrawn to your left hip. (Photo 17).

CHAPTER 6

THE PRINCIPLE OF BLOCKING AFTER ATTACKING

INTRODUCTION

In chapter five, we saw that with practice a karate man can develop skill in blocking his opponent's attack and then immediately countering with an attack of his own. Logically, therefore, we must develop our repertoire of karate skills so that we can with confidence face an opponent who has acquired this kind of skill. The only way to develop this repertoire is to include in it the ability to block the attacking techniques of the opponent which he uses after blocking your attacking techniques.

This is not an easy thing to do, as after putting the degree of concentration into an attacking technique which one has to if one would score with it, it is difficult then suddenly, on finding that one's technique has been blocked and that one is also being attacked, to tear one's attention from one's first intention and also to change one's physical posture in order to defend oneself. But with practice it can be done.

There are of course many double technique combinations comprising first an attacking technique followed by a blocking technique, and with practice and a little use of the imagination you will soon realize what these are. We have chosen the techniques illustrated in the following pages to illustrate this principle.

NOTE: In this chapter we shall be using techniques previously introduced, with one exception. This is 'shita-kentsui-uke' - downward fist-hammer block. This is used as the second technique in the second combination of techniques. It will be formally introduced and the reason for delay in introducing it is because its usefulness can best be demonstrated in the context in which it appears in this chapter.

Right Oi-Zuki & Right Soto-Ude-Uke

TECHNICAL DESCRIPTION

Face your opponent, each of you in the free-fighting stance. Assume your opponent has blocked your high Right Lunge Punch with a Left Rising Block. (Photo 2). If your opponent then uses as his counter-attack a high Reverse Punch, you can effectively block his counter by using a high Right Outer Forearm Block. (Photo 3).

Right Mae-Geri-Kekomi & Right Shita-Kentsui-Uke

INTRODUCTION

"Shita' means 'downward', 'ken' means 'fist', 'tsui' means 'hammer' and 'uke' means 'block.' This technique is the same as the second combination of techniques in chapter 3 called 'yoko'kentsui-uchi' - side fist-hammer strike, apart from the fact that it is used as a block instead of a strike and is aimed downwards instead of to the side.

TECHNICAL DESCRIPTION

Face your opponent, each in the free-fighting stance, (Photo 1 Chapter 6). Assume your opponent has blocked your right Front Thrust Kick with a Left Downward Block, (Photo 4). If your opponent then uses as his counter attack, say a Right Reverse Punch aimed at the level of your solar plexus, you can effectively block this counter by using a Right Downward Fist-Hammer Block. Do this by pushing your right fist forward and up and twisting it anti-clockwise, so that the little-finger side of the fist faces down. Then, without pausing, bring the muscular part of the little-finger side of your right clenched fist forcefully down on top of the forearm of your opponent's punching arm, thereby halting the progress of the punch towards you. (Photo 5).

Left Mawashi-Geri & Left Age-Uke

TECHNICAL DESCRIPTION

Face your opponent, each of you in the free-fighting stance as in Photo 1 Chapter 6. Assume your opponent has blocked your high Left Roundhouse Kick with a Right Back-Arm Sweeping Block (Photo 6). If your opponent then uses as his counter-attack a Left Jab to your face, you can effectively block his counter attack by using a Left Rising Block (Photo 7).

Left Yoko-Geri-Kekomi & Left Gedan-Kake-Uke

TECHNICAL DESCRIPTION

Face your opponent in the free-fighting stance as before. Assume your opponent has blocked your low Left Side Thrust Kick with a Left Hand Sweeping Block (Photo 8). If your opponent then uses as his counter attack a Left Roundhouse Kick to your mid-section, you can effectively block his counter attack by using a Left Downward Hooking Block (Photo 9).

Left Yoko-Geri-Kekomi & Left Ude-Barai

TECHNICAL DESCRIPTION

Assume the free-fighting stance as before. Your opponent has blocked your low Left Side Thrust Kick with a Left Scooping Block (Photo 10). If your opponent then uses as his counter attack a Left Roundhouse Punch you can effectively block his counter attack by using a Left Forearm Sweep (Photo 11).

Right Ushiro-Geri-Kekomi & Right Te-Nagashi-Uke

TECHNICAL DESCRIPTION

Both you and your opponent are in the free-fighting stance. Assume that your opponent has blocked your Right Back Thrust Kick with a Left Forearm Sweep (Photo 12). If he then uses as his counter-attack a Right Close Punch, you can effectively block his counter attack by using a Right Hand Sweeping Block (Photo 13).

12

13

CHAPTER 7

THE PRINCIPLE OF THE FEINT

INTRODUCTION

"Feinting" is a very important art to the karate man. It is dealt with in this chapter. Feinting is concerned with deceiving an opponent into believing that you intend to do one thing when in fact you intend to do something else; a karate man is at a serious disadvantage without this skill. The object of feinting is to cause your opponent to concentrate his defensive mechanism on a spot which is different from that which you intend to attack or use. This makes it much easier to succeed with your intended attack.

To succeed with feinting requires a great deal of thought on the kind of techniques which you include in your repertoire, and also that your favourite techniques work well with one another. You must be able, without any dithering or violent re-allocation of your concentration or posture, to move in a very well-oiled fashion from one technique to another. This is of course in the final analysis the acid test, as it were, of a karate man's bag of techniques.

Two techniques are needed in a "feinting operation". One will be used in the actual feint and the other to take advantage of the opponent's reactions. Theoretically, any two techniques will suffice. In reality, certain combinations of techniques work much better than any others. This is because certain movements lend themselves more to being used harmoniously together than do others. These combinations can be discovered with hard practice and intelligent thought but this takes time and it is the object of this book to considerably reduce this time with the following examples and advice.

To "con" your opponent into reacting suitably to your first feint, the first technique must be begun with great speed, power, and naturalness, in a confident manner, so that he will be taken in. Your second "true' attacking technique must have the same qualities so that your opponent will not have time to realise his mistake and rectify it.

The technical combinations which follow can be built up into very effective feinting sequences. The list is not exhaustive but is sufficient to occupy you for quite some considerable time, as combining techniques in this way for feinting purposes requires a lot of practice. If you attempt to include too many of these combinations in your repertoire too quickly you will defeat your own object which is to confuse your opponent and you will end up instead by confusing **yourself.** So until you have got a clear idea by practicing and improving your ability with the following combinations of feinting techniques, do not go on to developing others which your training and common sense will suggest to you.

NOTE: This chapter will make use only of the techniques which have already been introduced.

Right Oi-Zuki & Left Mae-Geri-Kekomi

TECHNICAL DESCRIPTION

Face your opponent, each of you in the free-fighting stance (Photo 1). Feint with a Right Lunge Punch as though you intended to punch your opponent's face (Photo 2). Instead of delivering the punch you quickly and smoothly deliver a Left Front Thrust Kick to his body (Photo 3).

Right Oi-Zuki & Left Mawashi-Geri

TECHNICAL DESCRIPTION

From the free fighting stance (Photo 1 Chapter 7) you feint with a Right Lunge Punch as though to hit your opponent's face (Photo 4). Instead of delivering the punch, quickly and smoothly deliver a Left Roundhouse Kick to his body (Photo 5).

Right Oi-Zuki & Right Yoko-Geri-Kekomi

TECHNICAL DESCRIPTION

Assume the free-fighting stance and feint with a Right Lunge Punch to the opponent's face (Photo 6). Instead of delivering the punch you quickly and smoothly deliver a Right Side Thrust Kick to his body (Photo 7).

Right Ushiro-Geri-Kekomi & Left Yoko-Geri-Kekomi

TECHNICAL DESCRIPTION

Face each other in the free-fighting stance and you feint with a Right Back Thrust Kick (Photo 8). Instead of delivering this kick, quickly and smoothly deliver a Left Side Thrust Kick (Photo 9).

Left Yoko-Geri-Kekomi & Right Ushiro-Geri-Kekomi

TECHNICAL DESCRIPTION

Assume the free-fighting stance and feint as though to strike your opponent with a Left Side Thrust Kick (Photo 10). Instead of this kick you quickly and smoothly put your left foot to the ground and deliver a Right Back Thrust Kick (Photo 11).

Left Mawashi-Geri & Right Mae-Geri-Kekomi

TECHNICAL DESCRIPTION

Face your opponent, each of you in the free-fighting stance, and then feint with a Left Roundhouse Kick (Photo 12). Instead of delivering this kick, quickly and smoothly put your foot to the ground and deliver a Right Front Thrust Kick (Photo 13).

Right Mae-Geri-Kekomi & Right Oi-Zuki

TECHNICAL DESCRIPTION

Both assume a free-fighting stance and then feint with a **Right Front Thrust Kick** as though aiming it low. Then, instead of delivering this kick, quickly and smoothly get your right foot to the ground and deliver a **Right Lunge Punch** to the opponent's face, (Photo 15).

14

15

Right Oi-Zuki & Left Gyaku-Zuki

TECHNICAL DESCRIPTION

From the free-fighting stance you feint as if to deliver a **Right Lunge Punch** (Photo 16). Instead of delivering this punch, quickly and smoothly extend your right fist further forward as you bend your left arm more, and stepping further forward with your right foot, deliver a **Left Reverse Punch** (Photo 17).

16

17

INTRODUCTION

Although in Karate one must concentrate mostly on striking and defensive-blocking techniques, and evasions as described already, one should develop skill also in the throwing techniques which can be brought off in a karate situation.

Of course if you manage to secure a controlling hold on your opponent's jacket, you can execute any of the classical judo throwing techniques which you may have learned from judo training. However, you must never lose sight of the fact, when doing karate free-fighting, that in the vast majority of situations which occur you would have great difficulty in securing a hold on your opponent strong enough or quickly enough to enable you to throw him before he scored against you with a punch, kick, etc., which can be done with a lot of speed.

This is not to say that if one has judo experience one should give up any idea of using throwing techniques for the execution of which one must needs get a hold on one's opponent's jacket with both hands. But, it is necessary to face the fact that opportunities for using this type of throw are quite rare in karate free-fighting, especially against an experienced karate man. What one should do therefore from the point of view of using throwing techniques in free-fighting is to develop a repertoire of throwing techniques for which one gets plenty of opportunities, even in free-fighting, without the risk of being scored against by one's opponent before one can finish the throw. The following examples are the main throws of this kind which will be described and illustrated in this chapter: 'de-ashi-barai', 'kube-nage' and 'sode-nage'.

STRIKING AFTER THROWING

In karate, as one must follow up any throwing technique with some kind of striking, punching or kicking technique in order to score a point, one must also develop skill in delivering a technique of this kind after completing throwing one's opponent. The most widely used techniques for this purpose are the following, which will be illustrated in the articles on throwing techniques: 'shta-zuki', 'shta-geri', 'shta-shuto-uch', 'shta-kentsui-uchi', 'shta-empi-uchi'.

None of these techniques has been used in previous chapters. We shall, therefore, formally introduce them. In this case we shall introduce them now, in one section and not along with the throws, so that you can study them separately and then be able to give the throwing techniques your full attention without being distracted by these new striking methods. After all, throwing techniques are what this chapter is mainly concerned with.

The striking techniques used after the throws will of course be described technically in the same articles as on the throws. But, we repeat, we think it better to give the formal introduction of the new striking techniques here.

CHAPTER 8

THE PRINCIPLE OF THROWING

INTRODUCTION TO SHTA-ZUKI (DOWNWARD PUNCH)
'Shta' means downward, and 'zuki' means 'punch'. The name of the technique refers to the fact that when we apply it we punch downward at an opponent, usually after having thrown him. This technique is simply a Reverse Punch or Jab directed downward.

INTRODUCTION TO SHTA-GERI (DOWNWARD KICK)
As you already know, 'Shta' means 'downward'; 'Geri' means 'kick'. The name of this technique refers to the fact that when we apply it, we kick downward at the opponent, usually after throwing him.

INTRODUCTION TO SHTA-SHUTO-UCHI (DOWNWARD KNIFE HAND STRIKE)
As you already know, 'Shta' means 'downward'; 'Shuto' means 'knife hand'; 'Uchi' means 'strike'. The name of this technique refers to the fact that we simply use a Knife Hand Strike aiming it downward.

INTRODUCTION TO SHTA-KENTSUI-UCHI (DOWNWARD FIST HAMMER STRIKE)
The only word you need reminding about here is 'kentsui': 'ken' means 'fist', and 'tsui' means 'hammer'. Here we simply use a Fist Hammer Strike aiming it downward.

INTRODUCTION TO SHTA-EMPI-UCHI (DOWNWARD ELBOW STRIKE)
As you already know, 'Shta' means 'downward'; 'Empi' means 'elbow'; 'Uchi' means 'strike'. The name of this technique refers to the fact that we simply use an Elbow Strike aiming it downward. In this case, the striking surface is the back of the elbow, unlike the case of the Roundhouse Elbow Strike where the striking surface is the front of the elbow.

De-Ashi-Barai

INTRODUCTION

'De' means 'advanced', 'ashi' means 'foot' and as you know 'barai' means 'sweep'. With this technique we throw the opponent by sweeping away from under him his advanced foot with the sole of the foot.

TECHNICAL DESCRIPTION

Face your opponent as in photo 1. Stretch your right foot forward and to the left and slightly to the rear of your opponent's left foot, and bringing the sole of your right foot forcefully towards the rear left corner of the opponent's lower left heel, sweep his left foot from under him in a diagonal direction (Photo 2). These actions will throw the opponent on to his back in front of you. Your position then enables you to follow up the throw with speed and naturalness with Left Shta-Zuki (Downward Punch). Do this by simply placing your right foot to the ground in front of you, extending your right hand and withdrawing your left hand to prepare for the punch, then directing a Left Reverse Punch downwards at your opponent's face or chest as you lower your body by bending both knees. (Photo 3).

TECHNICAL DESCRIPTION OF DE-ASHI-BARAI DONE WITH THE LEFT FOOT AGAINST THE OPPONENT'S RIGHT FOOT.

An excellent opportunity to apply the Left Advanced Foot Sweep is when the opponent uses a Right Lunge Punch against you. Face your opponent, each of you in the free-fighting stance and as the opponent has almost completed a Right Lunge Punch against you, do a Grasping Block against the sleeve of his punching arm, and with the sole of your left foot apply the Advanced Foot Sweep against the rear right corner of the opponent's lower right heel in a diagonal direction (Photo 4).

The sweeping action combined with a downward pull on his right sleeve with your left hand will cause the opponent to be thrown on to his back in front of you. In this case as in the previous article you can speedily and naturally apply a Downward Punch after completing the throw, in this case using a Right Downward Punch instead of a Left and also controlling the opponent with your left hand grasp on his right sleeve as you deliver the punch.(Photo 5). When you do the punch you may either go down on your knee as in photo 5 or keep the knee off the ground as in photo 3.

We should like to describe and illustrate here the technique Shta-Geri (Downward Kick) which is a good alternative in this case to a Downward Punch for following up the throw with a strike.

Do this by placing your foot (left) to the ground after the throw as you continue to control your opponent with your left hand grasp on his sleeve, and then raising your right foot in the air. (Photo 6). Then, without pausing, aim the bottom of your right heel at your supine opponent by forcefully straightening your right leg downwards while twisting it ninety degrees anticlockwise as you pivot to your left on your left foot. The power of this kick is augmented if, at the same time as you kick, you stretch your opponent's body by pulling him up with your left hand grasp on his right sleeve. (Photo 7).

NOTE: Though the way described is considered to be the strongest way to deliver a Downward Kick, it can also be delivered with quite a lot of power without twisting the leg or pivoting on the left foot but by simply straightening the leg forcefully downwards. (Photo 8). This style of downward kicking is often preferred as it can be done with slightly more speed. Practice both methods.

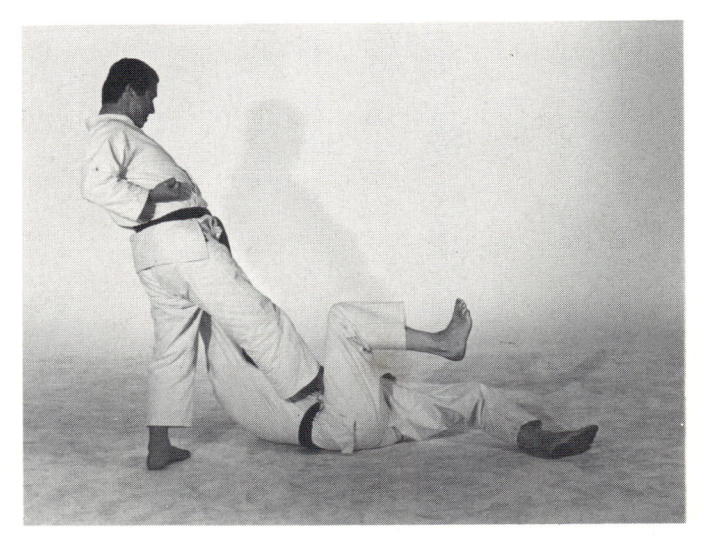

Kube-Nage

INTRODUCTION

'Kube' means 'neck' and 'nage' means 'throw'. The name of this technique refers to the fact that we apply it by encircling the opponent's neck with our arm then throwing.

TECHNICAL DESCRIPTION

An excellent opportunity to apply the Neck Throw is when the opponent uses a Left Front or Side Thrust Kick or a Left Roundhouse Kick to your mid-section. Face your opponent in the free-fighting stance, and first block your opponent's left kick with a left Scooping Block and pull his leg past the left side of your body to your left rear. (Photo 9). Continue to pull his leg to your left rear, bringing the upper part of his body close to your left side, where you must then release your grasp with your left hand on his left leg and encircle his neck from the front with your left arm (Photo 10). From the position shown in Photo 10 it is quite an easy matter to throw the opponent on to his back by pressing him backwards and downwards with your left arm hold on his neck and lowering your body to the ground, so that your left knee touches the ground, your right knee is kept off the ground, and the sole of your right foot is kept flat on the ground. (Photo 11).

The follow up striking techniques commonly used after completing this throw are the following: Shta-Shuto-Uchi(Downward Knife Hand Strike), (See photos 12 and 13 in Chapter 8); Shta-Kentsui-Uchi(Downward Hammer Fist Strike), (See photos 14 and 15 Chapter 8); and Shta-Empi-Uchi(Downward Elbow Strike), (See photos 16 and 17 Chapter 8).

12

13

14

15

16

17

83

Sode-Nage

INTRODUCTION

"Sode" means 'sleeve' and 'nage' means 'throw'. This refers to the fact that when we apply it we control the opponent with a grasp on his sleeve in order to throw him.

TECHNICAL DESCRIPTION

Face your opponent in the free-fighting stance. The opportunity for applying the Sleeve Throw occurs when you have managed to block your opponent's RIGHT Lunge Punch by applying a Left Grasping Block against the under part of his right sleeve. (Photo 18). After securing the grasp on the opponent's right sleeve with your left hand, quickly start pushing his right arm upwards as you rapidly rotate your body clockwise, placing, in almost one action, your right foot close to your opponent's right foot and your left foot past his left foot, so that both of your feet are pointing forward with your back towards the opponent and with the lower part of the back of your left calf blocking the front of his left shin, (Photo 18).

Then, with your grasp on his right sleeve with your left hand, push the opponent up and forwards across your left leg, then finally push him down and forwards in order to throw him on to his back (Photo 20).

After this throw, you are conveniently positioned in relation to your opponent to apply a Right Downward Punch, but this time with the fist on the same side as the foot in front, unlike the previous two illustrations of this technique which were done with the fist on the same side as the foot behind. In other words, this time you do a Right Kizami-Zuki (Jab) downwards, preferably while continuing to control the opponent on the ground with your left hand grasp on his right sleeve. (Photo 21).

LIST OF JAPANESE TERMS USED TO DESCRIBE KARATE STANCES AND TECHNIQUES

DACHI (STANCE)
- Fudo-Dachi (Rooted Stance)
- Hachiji-Dachi (Open-Leg Stance)
- Hangetsu-Dachi (Wide Hour Glass Stance)
- Heisoku-Dachi (Informal Attention Stance)
- Jiyu-Dachi (Free-Fighting Stance)
- Kiba-Dachi (Straddle Leg Stance)
- Kokutsu-Dachi (Back Stance)
- Musube-Dachi (Informal Attention Stance, Feet Turned Out)
- Neko-Ashi-Dachi (Cat Stance)
- Renoji-Dachi (L Stance)
- Sanchin-Dachi (Hour-Glass Stance)
- Shiko-Dachi (Square Stance)
- Shizen-Dachi (Natural Stance)
- Sochin-Dachi (Diagonal Straddle Stance)
- Teiji-Dachi (T Stance)
- Uchi-Hachiji-Dachi (Inverted Open-Leg Stance)
- Zenkutsu-Dachi (Forward Stance)

TSUKI-WAZA (PUNCHING TECHNIQUES)
- Age-Zuki (Rising Punch)
- Awase-Zuki (U-Punch)
- Choku-Zuki (Straight Punch)
- Gyaku-Zuki (Reverse Punch)
- Hasami-Zuki (Scissors Punch)
- Heiko-Zuki (Parallel Punch)
- Hiraken-Zuki (Fore-Knuckle-Fist Straight Punch)
- Ippon-Ken-Zuki (One-Knuckle-Fist Straight Punch)
- Kagi-Zuki (Hook Punch)
- Kizami-Zuki (Jab)
- Mawashi-Zuki (Roundhouse Punch)
- Morote-Zuki (Double-Fist Punch)
- Nagashi-Zuki (Flowing Punch)
- Nakadate-Ippon-Ken-Zuki (Middle Finger One-Knuckle-Fist Straight Punch)
- Oi-Zuki (Lunge Punch)
- Shta-Zuki (Downward Punch)
- Tate-Zuki (Vertical-Fist Punch)
- Teisho-Zuki (Palm-Heel Punch)
- Ura-Zuki (Close Punch)
- Yama-Zuki (Wide U-Punch)

KERI-WAZA (KICKING TECHNIQUES)
- Fumikiri (Cutting Kick)
- Fumikomi (Stamping Kick)
- Gyaku-Mawashi-Geri (Reverse Roundhouse Kick)
- Hitsui-Geri (Knee Kick)
- Hizagashira-Geri (Knee Kick)- Same as Hitsui-Geri)
- Kesa-Geri (Diagonal Kick)
- Mae-Geri-Keage (Front Snap Kick)
- Mae-Geri-Kekomi (Front Thrust Kick)
- Mae-Tobi-Geri (Jumping Front Kick)
- Mawashi-Geri (Roundhouse Kick)
- Mikazuki-Geri (Crescent Kick)
- Nidan-Geri (Double Jump Kick)
- Shta-Geri (Downward Kick)
- Shta-Zuki (Downward Punch)
- Ushiro-Geri-Keage (Back Snap Kick)
- Ushiro-Geri-Kakomi (Back Thrust Kick)
- Ushiro-Mawashi-Geri (Back Roundhouse Kick)
- Yoko-Geri-Keage (Side Snap Kick)
- Yoko-Geri-Kekomi (Side Thrust Kick)
- Yoko-Tobi-Geri (Jumping Side Kick)

UCHI-WAZA (STRIKING TECHNIQUES)
- Empi-Uchi (Elbow Strike)
- (Mae-Empi-Uchi (Forward Elbow Strike)
- (Mawashi-Empi-Uchi (Roundhouse Elbow Strike)
- (Otoshi-Empi-Uchi (Downward Elbow Strike)
- (Shta-Empi-Uchi (Downward Elbow Strike) This is the same as Otoshi-Empi-Uchi.
- (Tate-Empi-Uchi (Upward Elbow Strike)
- (Ushiro-Empi-Uchi (Rear Elbow Strike)
- (Yoko-Empi-Uchi (Side Elbow Strike)
- Haishu-Uchi (Back-Hand Strike)
- Haito-Uchi (Ridge Hand Strike)
- Hiji-Uchi (Elbow Strike) This is the same as Empi-Uchi.
- Hiraken-Uchi (Fore Knuckle Fist Strike)
- Ippon-Ken-Uchi (One-Knuckle-Fist Strike)
- Kentsui-Uchi (Fist-Hammer Strike)
- Koko-Uchi (Tiger Mouth Hand Strike)
- Kumade-Uchi (Bear Hand Strike)
- Nakadate-Ippon-Ken-Uchi (Middle Finger One-Knuckle-Fist Strike)
- Seiryuto-Uchi (Ox-Jaw Hand Strike)
- Shuto-Uchi (Knife Hand Strike)
- Shutsui-Uchi (Hand-Hammer Strike) This is another name for Kentsui-Uchi.
- Teisho-Uchi (Palm Heel Strike)
- Tetsui-Uchi (Iron Hammer Strike) This is also another name for Kentsui-Uchi.
- Uraken-Uchi (Back-Fist Strike)

UKE-WAZA (BLOCKING TECHNIQUES)
- Age-Uke (Rising Block)
- Ashibo-Kake-Uke (Leg Hooking Block)
- Ashikubi-Kake-Uke (Ankle Hooking Block)
- Deai-Osae-Uke (Pressing Block Stepping In)
- Gedam-Barai (Downward Block)
- Gedan-Kake-Uke (Downward Hooking Block)
- Gedan-Uke (Downward Block) This is the same as Gedan-Barai.
- Haishu-Uke (Back-Hand Block)
- Haiwan-Nagashi-Uke (Back-Arm Sweeping Block)
- Hiji-Suri-Uke (Elbow Sliding Block)
- Jodan-Age-Uke (Rising Block) This is the same as Age-Uke.
- Juji-Uke (Cross (x) Block)
- Kake-Shuto-Uke (Hooking Knife-Hand Block)
- Kakiwake-Uke (Reverse Wedge Block)
- Kakuto-Uke (Bent-Wrist Block)
- Keito-Uke (Chicken Head Wrist Block)
- Kentsui-Uke (Fist-Hammer Block)
- Maeude-Deai-Osae-Uke (Forearm Pressing Block)
- Maeude-Hineri-Uke (Forearm Twist Block)
- Morote-Sukui-Uke (Two-Handed Scooping Block)
- Morote-Tsukamai-Uke (Two-Handed Grasping Block)
- Morote-Uke (Augmented Forearm Block)
- Nami-Ashi (Inside Snapping Block)
- Seiryuto-Uke (Ox Jaw Hand Block)
- Shuto-Uke (Knife-Hand Block)
- Shutsui-Uke (Hand-Hammer Block) This is another name for Kentsui-Uke.
- Sokumen-Awase-Uke (Side Two Hand Block)
- Sokutei-Mawashi-Uke (Circular Sole Block)
- Sokutei-Osae-Uke (Pressing Block With Sole)
- Sokuto-Osae-Uke (Pressing Block With Foot Edge)
- Soto-Ude-Uke (Outer Forearm Block)
- Sukui-Uke (Scooping Block)
- Tate-Shuto-Uke (Vertical Knife-Hand Block)
- Teisho-Awase-Uke (Combined Palm-Heel Block)
- Teisho-Uke (Palm-Heel Block)
- Tekubi-Kake-Uke (Wrist-Hook Block)
- Te-Nagashi-Uke (Hand Sweeping Block)
- Te-Osae-Uke (Hand Pressing Block)
- Tetsui-Uke (Iron Hammer Block) This is also another name for Kentsui-Uke.
- Tsukamai-Uke (Grasping Block)
- Uchi-Ude-Uke (Inner Forearm Block)
- Ude-Barai (Forearm Sweeping Block)

List of Japanese terms used to describe karate stances and techniques   Continued.

YOKERU-KOTO   (EVASIONS)
Hidari-Naname-Ni-Yokeru-Koto   (Left Diagonal Evasion)
Migi-Naname-Ni-Yokeru-Koto   (Right Diagonal Evasion)
Ushiro-Ni-Yokeru-Koto   (Retreating Evasion)

NUKITE-WAZA   (SPEAR HAND OR POKING TECHNIQUES)
Ippon-Nukite   (One Finger Spear Hand)
Nihom-Nukite   (Two Finger Spear Hand)
Yonhon-Nukite   (Spear Hand)

LIST OF JAPANESE WORDS AND EXPRESSIONS
in common use in karate

Ai-Uchi (Simultaneous scoring with no points given).
Awashite (Combine or Plus).
Chudan (Middle level)
Chui (Warning)
Dame Desu (That's no good)
Dan (Degree)
Dan-Zuki (Consecutive punching with the same hand)
Deshi (Disciple, Trainee)
Dojo (Gymnasium)
I Desu (That's good)
Gedan (Lower level)
Geta (Iron Training clogs)
Gohon-Kumite (Form of basic sparring using five successive attacks)
Gyaku-Ashi (The rear leg)
Hajime (Start)
Hanmi (Half-front-facing position)
Hansoku (Disqualification, Foul)
Hantei (Decision)
Heian Shodan (First Kata of Fundamentals)
Heian Nidan (Second Kata of Fundamentals)
Heian Sandan (Third Kata of Fundamentals)
Heian Yondan (Fourth Kata of Fundamentals)
Heian Godan (Fifth Kata of Fundamentals)
Hidari (Left. In the sense of being opposite to Right)
Hikewake (Drawn Result)
Ippon (One or One point)
Ippon-Jiyu-Kumite (One attack semi-free sparring)
Ippon-Kumite (Form of basic one-attack sparring)
Jikan (Time off, or Time up)
Jiyu-Kumite (Free fighting)
Jodan (Upper Level)
Jogai (Outside of the contest area)
Kach (Win, or Win by)
Kamaite (Get into. Used with reference to stances)
Kata (Fixed sequence of techniques practised alone)
Karate-Gi (Karate kit)
Kia (Method of shouting peculiar to Japanese martial arts)
Kihon (Basic Training)
Kihon-Kumite (Basic prearranged sparring)
Kime (Focusing concentration and power)
Kokyu (Method of breathing)
Kumite (Sparring)
Kyu (Step in grading system)
Ma-Ai (Distancing)
Mae-Ashi (The front leg)
Mae-Ni-Ite (Going forward)
Mawate (Turn around, or about face)
Make (Loss, or Loss by)
Makiwara (Punching board)
Manaka-Ni-Haite (Come to the centre of the contest area)
Migi (Right. In the sense of being opposite to Left)
Nihon (Two, or Two Points)
Nihon-Geri (Two consecutive kicks)
Nihon-Zuki (Two consecutive punches)
Niren-Geri (Two consecutive kicks) This is the same as Nihon-Geri
Niren-Zuki (Two consecutive punches) This is the same as Nihon-Zuki
Os (Form of greeting peculiar to karate players in Japan)
Otagai-Ni-Rei (Bow to each other. The word Rei (Bow) is also used alone)
Renzoku-Geri (Combination kicking)
Renzuki (Alternative punching)
Sanbon (Three, or Three Points)
Sanbon-Geri (Three consecutive kicks)
Sanbon-Kumite (Form of basic sparring using three successive attacks)
Sanbon-Zuki (Three consecutive punches)
Sanren-Geri (Three consecutive kicks) This is the same as Sanbon-Geri
Sanren-Zuki (Three consecutive punches) This is the same as Sanbon-Zuki
Seito (Pupil, or Student)
Sensei (Teacher, instructor, professor, title of respect when addressing a person who teaches, instructs, etc. And when the word Sensei is used together with such a person's surname, the surname comes first and the word Sensei comes after it, i.e. Nakayama Sensei and not Sensei Nakayama)
Shiai (Contest)
Shiai-Jo (Contest Area)
Shimpan (Referee, Umpire, Judge)
Shobu (Match)
Shomen (Place for dignitaries)
Tsuyoi (Strong, Powerful)
Tsuzukete (Carry on, Continue)
Ushiro-Ashi (The rear leg) This is the same as Gyaku-Ashi
Ushiro-Ni-Ite (Going back)
Waza-Ari (Half point)
Yame (Stop)
Yoi (Get Ready)
Yowai (Weak)

Japanese numbers up to Ten
Ichi   One
Ni   Two
San   Three
Shi   Four
Go   Five
Roku   Six
Shichi Seven
Hachi Eight
Ku   Nine
Ju   Ten

Published by
PAUL H. CROMPTON LTD.
94, Felsham Road, London SW 15 1dq